EDUCATIONAL LEADERSHIP SIMPLIFIED

Sara Miller McCune founded SAGE Publishing in 1965 to support the dissemination of usable knowledge and educate a global community. SAGE publishes more than 1000 journals and over 800 new books each year, spanning a wide range of subject areas. Our growing selection of library products includes archives, data, case studies and video. SAGE remains majority owned by our founder and after her lifetime will become owned by a charitable trust that secures the company's continued independence.

Los Angeles | London | New Delhi | Singapore | Washington DC | Melbourne

BOB BATES
ANDY BAILEY

EDUCATIONAL LEADERSHIP SIMPLIFIED

A guide for existing and aspiring leaders

**$SAGE

Los Angeles | London | New Delhi
Singapore | Washington DC | Melbourne

SAGE

Los Angeles | London | New Delhi
Singapore | Washington DC | Melbourne

SAGE Publications Ltd
1 Oliver's Yard
55 City Road
London EC1Y 1SP

SAGE Publications Inc.
2455 Teller Road
Thousand Oaks, California 91320

SAGE Publications India Pvt Ltd
B 1/I 1 Mohan Cooperative Industrial Area
Mathura Road
New Delhi 110 044

SAGE Publications Asia-Pacific Pte Ltd
3 Church Street
#10-04 Samsung Hub
Singapore 049483

Editor: James Clark
Assistant editor: Rob Patterson
Production editor: Nicola Carrier
Marketing manager: Dilhara Attygalle
Cover design: Sheila Tong
Typeset by: C&M Digitals (P) Ltd, Chennai, India
Printed in the UK

Library of Congress Control Number: 2017944790

British Library Cataloguing in Publication data

A catalogue record for this book is available from
the British Library

ISBN 978-1-52642-376-4
ISBN 978-1-52642-377-1 (pbk)

At SAGE we take sustainability seriously. Most of our products are printed in the UK using FSC papers and boards.
When we print overseas we ensure sustainable papers are used as measured by the PREPS grading system.
We undertake an annual audit to monitor our sustainability.

CONTENTS

THE AUTHORS

Bob Bates was a Senior Executive in the Civil Service for twenty years. He is CEO of the Arundel Group and has been a management trainer in some of the country's most prestigious public and private sector organisations. He has been a teacher educator for the past fifteen years and has a PhD in Education, an MSc in Public Sector Management, and an MA in Education.

He is co-author of the international best-selling *The Little Book of Big Management Theories* (Pearson, 2013). This was the CMI's practical management book of the year in 2014. It was on WH Smith's non-fiction best-selling list for nearly a year and is being translated into ten languages. Bob has also written a best-selling book *The Little Book of Big Coaching Models* (Pearson, 2015). Books on *Learning Theories Simplified* and on *Special Educational Needs and Disabilities* were published by SAGE in 2016.

Andy Bailey was the Head Teacher of a primary school in Walsall in the West Midlands for twenty-six years from 1983 until 2009. From 2000 until 2005 he was an External Advisor for the national programme for the Performance Management of Head Teachers. He was a School Improvement Partner employed by the Birmingham and Walsall Education Authorities to work within a number of schools between 2006 and 2011. From 2012 until 2015 he was an inspector for Ofsted working as a Lead Inspector in 2014 and 2015. Since his retirement from his head teacher's post he has worked as a consultant in a number of primary schools in Birmingham and Walsall.

He has also written or co-written a number of educational publications for practitioners and pupils in England and Wales and the Caribbean and has lectured to teachers, managers and advisers in a number of local authorities and universities in England and also in the Caribbean.

INTRODUCTION

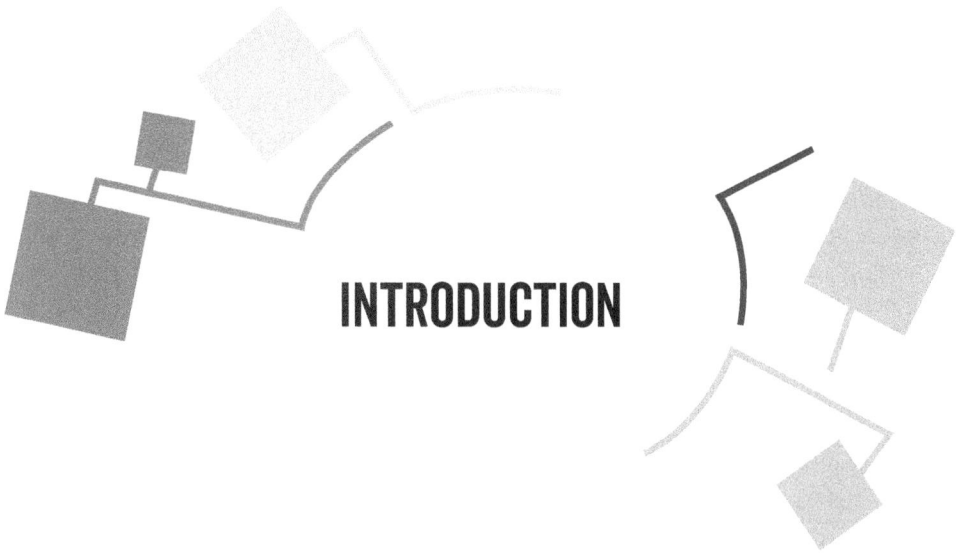

To be an excellent leader in today's education system, you need to merge an in-depth knowledge of education policy with proven best practices in organisational leadership and management. By reading this book you will not only understand the strengths and challenges of current public education policy, but will also be prepared to lead the organisations and initiatives that will create 21st-century systems of education that work for all learners.

It was no accident that the original formats of the Ofsted Inspection Handbooks and of Ofsted Reports on schools have been adjusted over years of national school inspections in recognition of the key role played by leadership in bringing about improvement within the educational system. The relentless drive by successive governments to raise standards in relation to those achieved by children around the world has recognised the crucial role played by leadership at different levels within schools in managing the plethora of initiatives designed to bring about the changes seen to be key to improving educational achievement and achieving economic prosperity.

In order for a leader to be regarded as effective their organisation, department or team will need to demonstrate success. In a climate, where the majority of published indicators relate to the achievement of learners in subjects such as English and mathematics this usually, though not exclusively, will mean academic success, measured in relation to national norms and expectations, which are consistently being ratcheted up.

What therefore makes a successful or outstanding leader in education? It would be so simple if there was a mould from which all aspirant leaders could be extracted. Unfortunately despite academics over the years providing a great number of very useful theories, these can nevertheless be quite complex, contradictory and often not applicable within the context of education leadership.

Whilst reports on schools in particular provide little detail on leadership styles there are certain words, such as 'high ambition, expectation and challenge', that feature consistently in Ofsted reports. The key question therefore is how the leader harnesses and utilises a multiplicity of personal qualities, skills and techniques to channel ambition constructively to achieve not only nationally recognised indicators of success but also those values and principles that the far-sighted leader has identified, particularly where these recognise and respond to the local context.

We aim to address this issue by combining the knowledge and understanding of the education leader's role with more general theories underpinning leadership and management to produce a model of excellence for those who are, or have aspirations to be, a leader within education. We are an experienced headteacher, with recent Ofsted Lead Inspector experience, and a writer of one of the UK's most recent successful management theory books, with over forty years' experience in public and private sector management.

Although the title suggests that leadership is a simple process it is far from that. The plethora of books on leadership theory, some of which are quite complex, demonstrate this. Many busy leaders in education simply don't have the time to plough through them to find answers to the problems they face in their organisation. What we have tried to do in this book is present a simple and concise appraisal of some of the theory that you can use to address the issues you may face in leading your organisation. We mix educational case studies with some drawn from industry and commerce, the world of sport and even a few trips to the cinema to offer a different perspective on the subject. We can assure you that all of the case studies, even the ones that you may find hard to believe, are real case studies with only the names and locations changed to protect the innocent, or in some cases the guilty.

Throughout the book we look at qualities that we feel characterise what professionalism in educational leadership is all about. Rather than just take these from the literature on the subject, they were suggested by a group of post-graduate educational students, mostly head teachers and senior managers, who were students on a Masters in Education programme. They wanted to call them *The 7 Habits of Highly Effective Head Teachers* or *The Magnificent Seven* but were worried about infringing copyright laws. With apologies to the great Freddie Mercury, they settled on the *Seven Cs of Why*. These are to be:

- Creative
- Courageous
- Challenging
- Communicative
- Confident
- Considerate
- Calm

Rather than use these qualities as chapter headings, we've gone for a more pragmatic approach in which the chapters denote issues that leaders have to deal with, such as managing teams, quality and time. The qualities will then be interwoven into each of the chapters, for example good team leaders need to be creative, courageous challenging and so on.

There was a lot of soul-searching to decide which theories to choose here and which ones to leave out, but the theories and models chosen will give you an interesting and powerful perspective on the qualities required to be a good leader.

A QUICK WORD ABOUT THE TERMINOLOGY WE USE THROUGHOUT THE BOOK

We use the term 'leader' to cover anyone involved in advancing and improving the educational processes in their organisation. This of course includes not just the head of the school (see below) or principal of a college or university or chief executive of a training venture but also those involved in the governance of the organisation, curriculum development and staff/student wellbeing.

The word 'organisation' covers schools, post-compulsory educational institutions and private training providers.

'Learners' are any pupils, students or trainees who attend the organisation.

'Staff' includes the teachers, lecturers, trainers, administrators and ancillary personnel who work for the organisation.

'Classroom' covers any environment where learning takes place.

'Session' is any bout of learning.

If you see the term 'curriculum leader' and your role is as a programme designer or course developer, then we don't think it's too great a leap of faith to recognise that the theories and models apply equally to you.

In respect of the terminology used, we did have problems in working out whether we should be using Head Teacher (acknowledging their teaching expertise), Headteacher (acknowledging their position of authority) or headteacher (as a general description). Even the Heads of school that were consulted with on this issue were ambivalent about what term to use. To avoid annoying anyone, we have opted to mix and match the terms.

Just a final word, we also use the term 'we' to describe our thoughts and experiences. It's important that the reader appreciates that this book is a joint effort and although we may not have shared a particular experience or agreed entirely on a particular issue, we had enough sense to compromise on that issue before committing to paper. The good news is that we still talk to one another and turn out three times a week to play football (of the fast walking variety).

1
LEADERSHIP AND MANAGEMENT

In the 2015 Department for Education's (DfE, 2015b) advice to headteachers, aspiring headteachers and governing bodies, they claim that headteachers, together with those responsible for governance, are guardians of the nation's schools. The DfE further claim that headteachers in particular:

- occupy an influential position in society and shape the teaching profession;
- are lead professionals and significant role models within the communities they serve;
- have values and ambitions that determine the achievements of schools;
- are accountable for the education of current and future generations of children;
- have a decisive impact on the quality of teaching and pupils' achievements in the five nations' classrooms;
- lead by example the professional conduct and practice of teachers in a way that minimises unnecessary teacher workload and leaves room for high quality continuous professional development for staff;
- secure a climate for the exemplary behaviour of pupils;
- set standards and expectations for high academic achievements within and beyond their own schools, recognising differences and respecting cultural diversity within contemporary Britain.

It's little wonder therefore that a significant part of the Ofsted inspection report is about leadership and management. Mess up on this and you can kiss goodbye to any chance of getting a good or outstanding grade. Mess up really badly and even good performance results may not save you from going into special measures. How therefore can you respond to the challenge of being an effective leader?

Reading McGrath and Bates (2017) *Little Book of Big Management Theories 2e* will give you over a dozen entries from which you can choose a leadership or management style that suits you. In this chapter of the book, we are going to summarise some of the popular ones, even throwing in a bit of the more controversial ideas on leadership and dispelling some of the myths about leadership. We are then going to give you something that will floor anyone who asks you a question about your leadership style. Hold on! Don't just jump to this, read the build-up to it.

Let's start by looking at the difference between leadership and management. There is a mass of literature covering the difference between leaders and managers. Most of this suggests that leaders and managers possess different characteristics and are psychologically very different people. The truth is that anyone who holds a senior position in any organisation has to combine the roles of leader and manager if they are to do their job effectively. We would suggest that if you want to distinguish between the two, then something like 80 per cent of the leader's role is inspirational and 20 per cent is aspirational and – wait for it – 20 per cent of the manager's role is inspirational and 80 per cent is aspirational. Okay, happy with this? Leaders have the vision about what kind of organisation they want to be the head of: managers have the responsibility for making it happen. Let's see if we can unravel this some more.

LEADERSHIP

Being an inspirational or visionary leader doesn't come easy and there is a debate about whether great leaders are born or made. The nature–nurture debate is an interesting one and there are examples of great leaders spawning awful leaders (e.g. Edward I and Edward II) and great leaders being born from humble beginning (such as Joan of Arc). We don't have a firm view on this issue. We can accept that there are genetic traits that may be passed down that will influence performance as a leader. We also believe that experience and learning are important in shaping good leadership.

Whatever your position is in the nature–nurture debate you need to be aware that there are many myths about leadership that have grown up over the years that may affect your thinking on the subject. Here are six myths covering intelligence, power, action, personality, style and expertise that we now want to consider.

MYTH # 1: YOU DON'T HAVE TO BE INTELLIGENT TO BE A GREAT LEADER

No, you haven't misread this. We are claiming that only intelligent people can be great leaders. We need to qualify what we mean here.

Intelligence has for many years been measured using intelligence quotient (IQ) tests. In more recent years, these tests have been criticised for failing to take account of the complex nature of the human intellect and the inference that there are links between intellectual ability and characteristics such as race, gender and social class. If your perception of intelligence is based on IQ tests, then we would suggest that there is no correlation between intelligence and the ability to lead.

Daniel Goleman (1996) suggested that intelligence is not just about developing a high IQ or being technically skilled, but that people also need to develop their emotional intelligence. He argued that there were five key elements of emotional intelligence, which we have interpreted for leaders. These are summarised as:

Self-awareness: Leaders must be aware of the relationship between their thoughts, feelings and action. They must be able to recognise what thoughts about a situation sparked off which emotions and the impact these emotions can have on themselves and those around them.

Managing emotions: Leaders must analyse what is behind these emotions and be able to deal with them in a positive manner.

Empathy: Leaders must also be able to deal with the emotions of those around them in a positive manner. This requires them to be able to understand more about the nature of any concerns being expressed about their leadership.

Social skills: Leaders need to develop quality relationships. This will have a positive effect on all involved. Knowing how and when to take the lead and when to follow is an essential social skill.

Motivation: Leaders can't always rely on external rewards to motivate others. They must support their staff to develop their own source of intrinsic motivators by encouraging them to appreciate what they can do and not to focus on the things they can't do.

Goleman argued that having a high level of self-awareness, and an understanding of others, makes you a better person as well as a better leader. He also argued that rather than losing brain cells through the aging process, the brain continuously reshapes itself in line with the experiences we have. Goleman suggested that by persisting with positive thoughts and actions your newly reformed brain will ensure that you will have a positive outlook in how you work as a leader and will result in you naturally doing the right thing for your followers, in the right way. Of course Goleman's theories are speculation. But don't they sound good and worth trying out.

If you agree, then here are some tips to help you:

- Develop your self-awareness by keeping a record of any key incidents that took place connected with your leadership. A simple note of what happened, why it happened, what you did and what impact it had on you and those around you will suffice.
- Try to look at the situation from your followers' perspectives. Although you may disagree with them, recognising that they are entitled to their views and beliefs will make you more understanding towards them and the problems they may be facing.

- Listen carefully to what others in your organisation (not just your staff but also the learners and their parents) have to say and never be afraid to re-examine your own values in light of what they have to say.
- Always try to find a win–win solution to any situation arising with you and your followers.

Although he has a popular following, critics of Goleman claim that he can only speculate that his theories on intelligence are any more valid than the reliance on IQ testing.

CASE STUDY

Lesley had not long been appointed as the curriculum leader for mathematics in her primary school when she set about trying to raise pupil achievement by implementing a published scheme of work that had proven effective in a number of other school settings.

She was disappointed when a year on from implementing the scheme there had only been a limited overall improvement in pupil achievement. Part of the evaluation she subsequently carried out focused upon the role that leadership and management had played in the relative lack of success of the initiative.

It became apparent that her analysis of the issue had been too superficial and had therefore failed to identify key factors contributing to low pupil achievement within the school. Consequently she concluded that the adopted solution (the published scheme), however effective in other settings that she had considered, may not have been the most appropriate for her school.

Despite exhaustive monitoring during the year, Lesley felt that there had been insufficient feedback to staff and a failure to communicate effectively with those members of staff who were charged with delivering the new initiative. Although they had been thoroughly familiarised with the scheme, and had received appropriate training and support materials, little account had been taken of such factors as the differing aptitudes and attitudes of the staff.

When Lesley examined her motives for implementing the change she concluded that at least in part they reflected a desire on her part to make an impact and prove her worth to others, in particular senior leaders. In adopting standard, rigid and inflexible targets Lesley had left little room for maneuver, which proved to have a demotivating effect on some staff and inhibited her capacity to empathise with others.

Lesley concluded that her leadership and management of the project was a prime cause of its relative lack of success. This helped to frame a strategy for the second year of the project and proved to be an important lesson for her professional development towards becoming a successful senior leader.

It's clear that Lesley's self-awareness was heightened by keeping a record of events that took place during her efforts to implement the change and the impact that it had on those involved. Her willingness to look at the situation from others' perspectives helped her to adopt a more successful strategy.

> **Hot Tip:** Be prepared to look at situations from other people's perspectives and never be afraid to re-examine your own values in light of what they have to say.

MYTH # 2: POWER CORRUPTS AND ABSOLUTE POWER CORRUPTS ABSOLUTELY

Of course, history is riddled with people who have abused the power they have been given or taken. Before we accept or reject this myth, we need to understand what we mean by power. There are numerous models of power. One of the most compelling was outlined by **John French** and **Bertram Raven** (1959). They identified five sources of power that a leader can call upon to encourage or compel compliance. These are:

Positional power: As a leader you hold a position of authority in the organisation. Identify the limits of that authority but act with confidence when you do exercise authority and expect staff to comply with your legitimate requests. Expect compliance and enforce it.

Reward power: As a leader you control key resources within your organisation. Identify the range of rewards you can give staff and remember they need not be financial. Public recognition or a private appreciation of a job well done may mean more to a person than promotion or a pay rise. Always deliver on any promises that you make to reward someone.

Coercive power: Some leaders will have reached the position they hold through force (physical or psychological). Identify the limits of your coercive power. Never use coercive power to bully people, but it is perfectly legitimate to deal forcibly with poor performance and apply a suitable sanction. Always carry through with any threats that you make to punish someone.

Expert power: Most leaders gain recognition as a leader because of their experience and expertise in the job. Identify what, if any, expert power you have. If you have a professional qualification you will per force have a degree of expert power. Continuously update specialist knowledge in one or more areas of your discipline and use it in your organisation.

Charismatic power: Some leaders gain recognition as a leader because of their charismatic hold over their followers. Remember that charisma is in the eye of the beholder. So think about how you appear to your staff. Act with confidence and integrity and they will think you have charisma.

French and Raven argue that leaders should work to accumulate as many sources of power as possible. Typically some degree of positional, reward and coercive power comes with the leadership role. Leaders need to test the limits of each and build up their expert power. As for charismatic power, that's something we all need to work on.

It's not the nature of power that corrupts therefore, even if this power is absolute and unchallenged, but the people who wield it. Both Hitler and Martin Luther King had a powerful hold over their followers, one used it for violent purposes the other to promote peaceful demonstrations.

Here are two cases of college principals that one of us has worked with who demonstrate the differences in exercising power.

CASE STUDY

Mary was a surprise choice to be the principal of a new community-based college formed out of the merger of two adult education centres that delivered vocational training throughout a network of community centres in the borough. She had ousted the incumbent principals of the two centres, who became her vice-principals. Many were impressed by Mary's talk of her vision for the new college and the values of openness and trust that she wanted to underpin the vision. She won everyone over with her charisma. In the space of three years, she took the college from an adequate institution to an outstanding one. But there was a price to pay for this. In a document that she marked 'Confidential – for management only' she wrote about her desire to take education provision away from community centres and into libraries. This would mean significant job losses and inconvenience for community-based learners who would have to travel further to attend classes. Staff morale was at an all-time low, with five cases of harassment being waged against her. Sickness due to stress was quadrupled.

Mary left after three years as principal during which time no members of the original nine-strong senior management team were still in post, seven out of the original ten community centres that delivered training had closed down and funding for community-based vocational training was reduced to less than a quarter of its previous level.

It's difficult to weigh up here whether power was being used for the good of all or in the interests of the individual wielding it. Mary's intention was always to leave after three years having taken the college to an outstanding grade. She achieved this, but at a price. On visiting the college regularly it's distressing to hear what people there are saying about morale and their concerns for the future of the college. Tom's college in the next case study no longer exists as a separate entity but even after fifteen years, he is still talked about with respect and affection.

CASE STUDY

Tom was the principal of a large FE college. He had worked his way up from an engineering instructor through to the principal's post. He was generally looked on as a bit of pragmatist whose philosophy was 'If it works, it's good'. He had a knack of finding resources to fund even the most outrageous ideas if he thought it would benefit his staff or learners. This never endeared him to inspectors, with the college never scoring highly for Leadership and Management and overall grades never better than good. He was, however, widely respected by staff and most people who came into contact with him. On one occasion, concerned that staff had nowhere to have a break from students, Tom gave up his office to them.

When he was asked where he would sit, he replied, 'In the classrooms or the canteen, anywhere where I can get the low-down on how we are doing and I don't get pestered every minute with phone calls and emails. If they want me they know where I'll be.' There never was a title to describe his leadership style and we doubt whether he would have thanked anyone who would have given him one.

Tom retired after twenty years in the same college. The college grades flitted between adequate and good (never inadequate or outstanding) and they merged with another college to form one of the country's largest further education colleges.

Hot Tip: Know what sources of power you have access to and identify who in your organisation exercises power and what you can learn from them.

MYTH # 3: THE MEANS DOESN'T JUSTIFY THE ENDS

The converse of this concept is usually attributed to Niccolo Machiavelli. Machiavelli was a 16th-century Italian writer, who, out of work and looking for a job, wrote a job application to the Magnificent Lorenzo de Medici. In the history of the world it was one of the longer job applications and was later published as *The Prince* (Machiavelli, 2004).

The Prince has become described by many as an amoral guide to leadership and the term 'Machiavellian' as being something that is characterised by deception and ruthlessness. Never one to avoid controversy, we're going to tease out a few extracts from *The Prince* that we hope will show Machiavelli in a different light, with some useful tips for leaders (please excuse the political incorrectness in the extracts – it was written in the 16th-century):

- **'There is no other way to guard yourself against flattery than by making men understand that telling you the truth will not offend you.'** Surround yourself with people who are not self-serving and will advise you honestly and challenge you.

- **'The first method for estimating the intelligence of a ruler is to look at the men he has around him.'** Never fool yourself, or allow anyone else to mislead you, about the reality of the situation you face. Only by confronting them and the reality can you deal with the present and plan for the future.
- **'Acknowledge the possibilities for failure: a skilful leader does better to act boldly than to try to guard against every possible eventuality.'** Don't be afraid of failure. Only those that do nothing never fail.
- **'Without an opportunity, their abilities would have been wasted, and without their abilities, the opportunity would have arisen in vain.'** Your staff are your most valuable resource, so make sure they are allowed every opportunity to develop themselves.
- **'It is not titles that honour men, but men that honour titles.'** Don't appoint people into the roles of Safeguarding Manager or Quality Manager in your organisation. Make safeguarding and quality themes that everyone in the organisation take responsibility for.
- **'All courses of action are risky, so prudence is not in avoiding danger but calculating risk and acting decisively.'** Don't be afraid to take calculated risks. The future is not set, but you can help shape it by your willingness to take risks and act with conviction.
- **'It must be considered that there is nothing more difficult to carry out, nor more doubtful of success, nor more dangerous to handle, than to initiate a new order of things.'** Never do anything illegal, but there will be occasions when you need to act in a ruthless manner in the interest of your organisation or your learners.
- **'He who becomes a Prince through the favour of the people should always keep on good terms with them; which it is easy for him to do, since all they ask is not to be oppressed.'** Be aware that anyone who helped you to reach a position of authority may see you as a threat. If this is a possibility, make yourself useful to them or plan your escape.

There was something of the fable of the Emperor's new clothes in the next case study. While people believed in Nick, he was able to wield power from a number of sources. He controlled resources within his team, had a steady stream of jokes and anecdotes that amused people and the support of senior staff within the university. Once the belief started to diminish, his jokes ceased to become funny and his disposition changed to one of intimidating others around him. He had forgotten the advice of Machiavelli that *'He who becomes a Prince through the favour of the people should always keep on good terms with them; which it is easy for him to do, since all they ask is not to be oppressed.'*

Remember, if you believe in this myth you are not the only Machiavellian in the world. They are evident in the policy makers, the managers in your organisation, the staff, the parents and even your learners. If need be, protect yourself against others who believe that the ends justify the means. They are unlikely to shy away from causing you problems if it suits their purpose. Remember that it's better to be useful to another Machiavellian than to be their friend.

CASE STUDY

Nick was something of an enigma. He reached the position of curriculum leader within the education faculty of a university via a training role within industry. He had a reputation for risky decision-making, which although causing concern amongst others in his department, who had a more traditional outlook on education, was bringing in a substantial amount of revenue for the department.

As Nick's reputation grew, so did the size of his team. He was given a lot of scope to recruit new members to his team whom he felt had a similar outlook to him. The team was immensely successful in the first year or two, bringing in a lot of work for the department in non-traditional areas such as the manufacturing and health sectors. Members of Nick's team were reveling in the praise and no-one, either inside or outside of the team, questioned Nick's decisions.

It may be that Nick felt that he was insulated from any criticism but, as one or two of his decisions backfired on him, he tried to blame the members of his team. A group of people that had once been in awe of Nick now began to question him and bit by bit, the team fell apart. Other curriculum leaders, who had been jealous of Nick's success, saw this as an opportunity to attack him in curriculum leaders' meetings.

Eventually, Nick's team was disbanded and he was moved into a more marginalised role where as his head of department claimed 'he could do less damage'.

Hot Tip: We're not advocating that you should always be deceitful or ruthless in what you do as an educational leader, but you should be able to play the game in the best interests of your staff and learners.

MYTH # 4: NICE PEOPLE DON'T MAKE SUCCESSFUL LEADERS

We work on the principle that leaders can only lead if people are prepared to follow them. In the two case studies above, we've looked at the power that leaders possess that might compel people to follow them. We guess that we all like nice guys (like Tom) as good human beings, but do they need something more (like Mary) to make them successful leaders?

The argument in favour of nice people making successful leaders is based on the feel-good assumption that the best leaders are collaborative, compassionate, empathetic and free of most defects of character. Opponents argue that the best human beings do indeed have these qualities, but the most successful leaders usually have something different. In this respect, they describe 'successful leaders' as being people who consistently show the ability to get things done, the ability to sell others an idea, the ability to talk their way out of a jam and the ability to bounce back from setbacks.

Nice people can make successful leaders. If you need proof – read the following case study.

CASE STUDY

Like many parents whose child is starting secondary school, Bob was concerned over whether he had made the right choice of school for his daughter, Amy. By the end of the first term all doubts had disappeared. Not only was his daughter doing well academically but she was a member of her school netball and rounders teams and was participating in the school orchestra. The icing on the cake was when the school staff performed a pantomime at Christmas, with the Head Teacher playing the arch villain.

Bob met his daughter's Head Teacher some three years after the Head had retired, and when he opened by saying 'You won't remember me but ...', the Head cut Bob short and said 'Of course I do, you're Amy's dad; how's she doing at university?'

Anthony Bryk and **Barbara Schneider** (2002) wrote about the importance of the social exchanges, such as that between Bob and his daughter's Head Teacher, that take place in a school community. They referred not just to what takes place in the classroom and staffroom but also to the relationships that develop with all stakeholders and their mutual dependency on each other to achieve desired outcomes. You don't get this by being nasty to people.

Bryk and Schneider refer to this principle as *relational trust*, and claim that this dependency is based on the obligations and expectations that people have of each other and can be categorised under the following headings:

Respect: This is marked by a leader's willingness to listen to what others are saying and a genuine commitment to take others' views into account.

Regard: This grows as a result of the leader being willing to extend themselves beyond the basic requirements of their role.

Competence: This can be measured by the confidence that everyone has in the leader's ability to lead.

Integrity: This is recognised through leaders behaving ethically and keeping promises.

Bryk and Schneider argue that *relational trust* cannot be taught, rather it occurs as a result of day-to-day exchanges and that even the simplest interactions can have a significant impact on building trust in the organisation. They suggest that educational leaders, managers and teachers have a key role to play in developing and sustaining relational trust. How they behave towards others, and the vision they have for their organisation, set the standards for respect and integrity.

Here are two lessons that can be learned from Bob's daughter's school:

- The Head Teacher embodied everything that is critical in relational trust. We've seen many Heads who *talked the talk* (their words were more impressive than their actions). Bob's daughter's Head Teacher was loved and respected by everyone in the school because he *walked the walk* (he believed actions spoke louder than words).
- Through their actions in extra-curricular activities, the staff at the school demonstrated their obligations to their pupils and their parents and each other. Through the pantomime, staff were interacting socially with each other, parents were acknowledging the extra effort staff were putting into rehearsals and pupils were seeing a different side to their teachers.

Of course, we accept that not all staff have the time in their busy caseloads to devote three months of their own time rehearsing for a one-off pantomime performance and that success should not be measured purely in terms of the time being spent by staff on such activities, but certainly, from a parent's perspective, this will do much to dispel any fears that parents have about their child's secondary education.

Whether you agree or disagree with the myth really depends on what you consider to be nice. There is a disease called *santaphobia*; a morbid fear of Father Christmas. Even Mother Teresa isn't exempt, as there is a phobia called *hagiaphobia*; a morbid fear of saintly people. Unless there is something called *Virginaphobia*, people like Richard Branson are living proof that nice people (most people think he's nice) do make good leaders. But, is Sir Richard the rule or a very rare exception? We could make a list of nice and nasty people who are proven good leaders, but we'll leave you to do that.

> **Hot Tip:** Be aware that the day-to-day exchanges, including even the simplest interactions, can have a significant impact on building trust and respect in the organisation.

MYTH # 5: LEADERS SHOULD HAVE THEIR OWN UNIQUE STYLE THAT THEY STRICTLY ADHERE TO

You probably read a lot about the importance of having the right style of leadership. Early on we mentioned the often asked question 'What is your style of leadership?'. We promised you an answer to floor the person asking you the question. Be patient, it's coming, but first here are some good responses from respected theorists that you might want to consider:

Action-centred leadership: John Adair (1983) argues that a leader must be concerned with the needs of the task, the individual and the team and that they must ensure that these different needs are met. Explain that you see your priorities as setting work standards, deadlines and targets and providing the resources and well-trained, motivated staff to achieve those targets.

Contingency leadership: Fred Fiedler's (1967) theory suggests that when you find yourself in an unfavourable situation you should change the situation not your leadership approach. This is suggested because it is assumed that leadership characteristics are psychological traits which are difficult to change. Explain that your priority is to identify the source of any problems you face and analyse how best to respond to them.

Situational leadership: Paul Hersey and Ken Blanchard (1969) suggest that as a leader you need to provide a combination of direction and support when dealing with a member of staff. Direction involves giving the person detailed instructions on how to complete the task/job. Support requires you to provide the encouragement and emotional support that they need to complete the task/job. Explain that your priority is to get to know and understand the people who work for you before deciding what level of support and direction is needed

Transactional leadership: James MacGregor Burns (1978) popularised the phrase 'transactional leadership'. It describes the, often informal, bartering process that goes on between leaders and staff all the time. He categorised these as: (a) constructive transactions, which involve the leader offering inducements to the follower to comply with their request; and (b) corrective or coercive transactions, which occur when the leader threatens the follower if they refuse to cooperate or if they fail to stop acting in a certain way. Explain that your priority is to get to know and understand the people who work for you before deciding whether they will respond better to offers of rewards or threats of punishments.

Distributed leadership: Today it has become nearly impossible for an individual to properly administer and lead any form of educational institution. Education leaders must assume responsibilities in an ever-wider range of areas: instruction, organisational culture, management, strategic development, budgeting, micro politics, human resources and external development. Any one leader will have difficulty successfully managing all these areas on his or her own and will need to delegate responsibilities. Cecil Gibb (1958), who is generally acknowledged as having coined the term 'distributed leadership', argues that securing staff members' full participation in the organisation's decision-making processes promotes meaningful collaboration and harmonious work relationships, generates passion for accomplishing goals, and boosts student and teacher productivity. Explain that your priority is to create and leave behind new leaders with the capability of serving their organisation and the wider community, and you can't fail to impress.

Here's a quick test: Which of the above leadership styles did the new Head in the following case study adopt?

CASE STUDY

Phil was the recently retired Head of a primary school in North Yorkshire and a hard act to follow. He was hard in many respects; his physical presence and aggressive nature meant that he was rarely challenged. His replacement, Simon, was a less imposing individual, both in terms of his size and nature. When Simon took over, Phil invited him out for a pint and told him not to take any nonsense from anyone, especially the parents.

Following an altercation between two parents in the playground, Simon stepped in to break up the argument. By now a crowd had gathered and, feeling that he needed to stamp his authority, Simon demanded that both parents apologise to each other. One of the parents shook his head and started to walk away. Simon told him to 'get back immediately'. As he continued to walk away, Simon repeated his demands. At this stage, the parent did return and punched Simon in the face.

It wasn't that Simon was wrong to intervene; indeed, it was important that he did. It was the aggressive way in which he did this that led to the unfortunate consequences. Simon had now lost any credibility and it was clear that it would take a lot to restore this.

We'd be surprised if you found any one of the listed styles that adequately described Simon's approach to leadership. There was certainly a bit of action-centred and contingency stuff in there, but nothing from the transactional style of leadership. Simon had clearly felt that he would gain respect by copying the previous Head's style of leadership. What he failed to do was to find out whether his predecessor was respected or feared.

If none of the entries in this section appeal to you, try 'chameleonistic leadership'. Tell anyone asking you what your leadership style is, that you adapt your style to suit the environment and circumstances you are in. Let's take a trip to the art gallery in the case study on the next page to see if we can unravel what we mean by this term.

Chameleon leadership is therefore predicated on the belief that when leaders make a decision, they must take into account all aspects of the current situation and act on those aspects that are key to the situation at hand. For example, if someone is leading staff during an Ofsted inspection, an autocratic style is probably best, where command and control may be necessary. If someone is leading on a programme to develop a more inclusive curriculum, a participative and facilitative leadership style is probably best, where cooperation and collaboration are vital.

Don't bother searching the web or buying McGrath and Bates's (2013) book or any other book on leadership to find out more about this form of leadership; it doesn't exist (yet) and will therefore floor anyone asking questions about your leadership style. Throwing in a bit of an art analogy, though, might confuse anyone who doesn't share your love of a particular art genre.

CASE STUDY

Derek had been a headteacher for over thirty years. He became poacher-turned-gamekeeper around the start of the millennium when he became an Ofsted inspector. Whenever he inspected a school, he would ask the headteacher to draw a quick illustration of their school in terms of leadership and management. Every picture was different. Derek saw: a ship with the head staring out to sea (figurehead?), a ship with the head at the wheel ('aye, aye captain'), a ship with the head on the bridge with binoculars ('I spy the promised land'), a ship with the head looking through his telescope with his blind eye ('I see no ships') and dozens more.

Derek found that this was a useful exercise and gave him an unprepared, from-the-gut insight into the school environment and school leadership. Not every headteacher participated in the exercise, with one head saying, 'If you ask me, the staff, the children, the parents, the Local Authority, you'll get a different picture from each!'

Derek found this exercise was always very enlightening and thought that Ofsted should have included this in their guidance! He told us that 'The secret is not to give the artist too much time to think, to anticipate what you are expecting and to make a neat job of it.' We can't resist including Derek's full thoughts on this (if art isn't your thing, then maybe skip over the next bit).

Derek told us, 'I think I might have alighted on a useful way of understanding some modern art. Just imagine the outcome of a Jackson Pollock work had he spent more time planning, for example choosing his palette range. Let's just consider this: Pollock's *Autumn Rhythm* was completed in his "Drip Period" and has been described as "chaotic" (kindly described, I must add). Every part of the work has equal significance, there being no focal point.'

We are left wondering if some of those sketches, now sadly consigned to the Ofsted shredder, were in fact the headteachers' contribution to abstract expressionism. Perhaps it is just better sometimes to say it as it is, or commit to your oeuvre quickly, or go with your first thought, reaction or response. We're not saying Pollock did this, but the headteachers being Ofsteded by Derek did. Why not have a go yourself (and remember to have a title)?

Hot Tip: Adapt your style of leadership to suit the environment and circumstances you are in.

MYTH # 6: YOU HAVE TO HAVE BEEN A GOOD TEACHER TO MAKE A GOOD HEADTEACHER

There is a shortage of good teachers wanting to become Headteachers. In some areas of the UK, between one-third and a half of all Heads will retire during the next five years which, with a shortage of suitable replacements, will create a crisis situation in the profession.

According to Malcolm Trobe, deputy general secretary of the Association of School and College Leaders, in an article in the *Guardian*, 'negativity and over-accountability have combined to mean that, especially in schools where there are extra pressures, it's much more difficult to attract candidates for job vacancies at the top'. Trobe adds that 'What you want are high-quality leaders,' he says. 'Bringing people in from outside is great if it works – but it can only be part of a programme, and the other part of the programme should be enabling good senior teachers to take on headship roles in schools – and that's what's missing at the moment' (Press Association, 2016).

Trobe also claims that 'Right now, good people are being turned off becoming Headteachers because the element of risk involved in the job has increased significantly. We're in a situation where the knee-jerk reaction is that if a school has problems, the answer is to get rid of the head. It's the football manager mentality, whereas what schools need is stability, and what heads need is constructive support, not the adversarial system we're in now where school inspections are hit-jobs.'

For Sion Humphreys, of the National Association of Head Teachers, also in an article in the *Guardian*, the crucial thing for outsiders coming into headships is the need to prove themselves: 'There have always been career shifters coming into education, and there's often a suspicion that hard economic times is part of what's fuelling that. It's not always the case, but these people do have to prove themselves in the classroom – they have to get professional credibility' (Moorhead, 2012).

CASE STUDY

Geoff was appointed head of a middle school in the South West. He had been a teacher for twenty years before becoming a Headteacher. He felt that it would be difficult for someone who had only been a teacher for a handful of years to go into a classroom and talk about learning pedagogy. When he sits down and observes lessons, teachers know he can do it because he's been a teacher for twenty years. Geoff doesn't object to appointing Headteachers from outside industry or commerce, or fast-tracking, but in terms of credibility he believes there's no substitute for teaching experience.

Although Geoff loves being a Headteacher he now recognises that more and more of his senior teaching colleagues think twice before applying for a headship. He questions who in their right mind is going to place themselves in the firing line to head up a school that needs improvement and undergoing the pressure when someone's livelihood is going to be determined by a two-day inspection. Geoff claims that many good senior teachers don't put themselves forward for the final step because they are smart enough to know that if they take that step and things go wrong, they could be out of a job.

The problem, which Geoff and others are facing, is that the current system is so adversarial that it puts the best applicants off. It makes observers go into a classroom and pick all the bad things you see going on there to use as a basis for improvement, instead of going in and look for the positive and then trying to build on it to make things even better. That's the approach the authorities need to take with schools and with headships because, while things are bad at the moment in terms of headteacher recruitment, it's possible that they're going to get a lot worse.

Future Leaders is a leadership development programme for those who share our commitment to eradicating educational disadvantage, and have the talent and commitment to become headteachers of schools in challenging contexts. The idea of *Future Leaders* is to identify people who were able and prepared to take on headships in the country's toughest schools – the ones that find it hardest to recruit leaders – and what *Future Leaders* always expected was that a proportion of those who applied to the scheme wouldn't come from traditional backgrounds.

Future Leaders' chief executive, Heath Monk, explains that the project wasn't conceived as a way of enticing those from other backgrounds into becoming heads, but over the five years it has been in existence, that has been one of the outcomes. He claims that, 'you don't have to have been a teacher for 20 years to be able to step up to these top jobs in tough schools.' The people that *Future Leaders* bring on board often have experience that turns out to be highly relevant to their work as heads, and, as Monk argues, 'far from being stale and not interested in reflection or change, they're brimming with enthusiasm and keen to bring in change' (Henshaw, 2016).

CASE STUDY

Colin enjoyed a successful career in the pharmaceutical industry before becoming a *Future Leader* and being appointed head of an independent school that focused on the needs of children at risk of being excluded. The school used creative and performing arts as a means of engaging with children. Although widely read in the arts and literature, Colin had no teaching experience in these subjects. What he did bring to the school was originality and a passion for working with governors, staff, learners and their parents to get them to challenge chronic under-achievement and tired attitudes to education.

Colin has been a head at the school for four years and many feel that he has bought an innovative approach to teaching in an environment that has been steeped in educational failure, neglect and low self-esteem.

So, what do you think? Do you need to have been a good teacher to make a good headteacher?

Someone who excels as a teacher may have demonstrated their love for their subject and have excellent subject knowledge. They may be able to deliver a lesson with pace and interest, use digital resources effectively, mark work efficiently and record those marks, know how best to teach tricky concepts and how to ask challenging questions of pupils in the most effective way. Finally, they need to have high expectations of their pupils and be determined to ensure that every pupil will master their subject.

Although these qualities set the scene for everything that's good in teaching, they may not be the ones looked for in a good headteacher, where the patience, tenacity and diplomacy to deal with awkward school governors, aggressive Ofsted inspectors or an uncooperative Local Authority, or the ability to conduct a charm offensive on a potential private sector investor, may be what's needed.

If you are an aspiring headteacher, contemplating an upward move, here are five factors to take into account:

- Don't fall into the trap of believing that competence or even excellence in your current role suggests that you will be competent in a higher-level role.
- Match your capabilities with the demands of the new job. Your starting point should be an analysis of the skills you already possess and those required to achieve success in the new role.
- Realise that it's not always necessary to gain satisfaction at work by seeking promotion because you are good in your existing job. Sometimes, without any significant change in your responsibilities, you can find a reward for your hard work through other incentives.
- If you have been promoted and discover that you are not competent at that level, additional training, mentoring or shadowing someone who is competent may give you the tools you need to succeed.
- If this doesn't work, never be afraid to revert back to your previous role. Your talent and skills were clearly appreciated at that level.

MANAGERS

By their nature all management theories are just a partial explanation and simplification of the complex reality they try to explain. To expect one theory to explain fully what is going on or to work in all situations is on a par with expecting that a map of the Moscow underground, with station names written in Cyrillic script, will help you navigate your way across the city (one of us tried it this year and got hopelessly lost).

Some theories that you read about will immediately appeal to you; others you will reject out of hand. That's fine. Some approaches won't suit your personality and unless they reflect your beliefs about how people should be treated you will find it difficult to use them effectively. What you should aim to do is take from each theory that which is useful to you. You can then combine it with aspects of other theories and your own personality and experiences to form your own unique management style. In the rest of this part of the book we summarise some of the great theories on management.

We start with the theorist who influenced early thinking on management practices that focus on the needs of the organisation before moving on to more contemporary models of management that focus on the needs of the individual.

Fredrick Winslow Taylor (1911) rose from shop-floor labourer to become a director at Bethlehem Steel, the largest steel maker in the United States. He was more interested in efficiency than the social aspects of managing people. His book *The Principles of Scientific Management* cemented his reputation as the father of scientific management. Here are three of Taylor's key management principles and how you can apply them:

Plan and control work: Review how each job is done in your team and ask the following questions: Do we need to do this job? Can it be done more efficiently? Does the work allocated to each member of staff match their abilities/strengths?

Use time-and-motion techniques: Regularly review the work that staff do and look for efficiency gains. Set deadlines and benchmarks for performance but don't sacrifice effectiveness for efficiency by relying exclusively on performance figures. Sometimes the quality of teaching isn't reflected in performance figures alone.

Carefully select and train staff: This was revolutionary at a time when most workers were given no formal training. It's now taken for granted that additional training can improve your team's productivity greatly. Make sure you have a well thought out process for identifying training needs and don't just rely on the annual performance review.

CASE STUDY

Ed's school had always had a deputy headteacher. However, when Tom, the long-serving deputy headteacher, decided it was time to improve his golf handicap by calling it a day it seemed an appropriate time for Ed to review the role. From the outset it was obvious that Tom was going to be a hard act to follow as over the years he had developed a vast repertoire of skills, practices and so on that it would be hard to replicate in one individual. Although individual prospective candidates offered great potential in specific areas, no one appeared to have the range and experience to undertake what under Tom's tenure had become a wide-ranging and very idiosyncratic role.

Ed's instinct was to innovate rather than try to replicate, redefining the roles and responsibilities of the senior leadership team and replacing the more general job of the Deputy Headteacher with two Assistant Heads who would undertake specific clearly defined roles, aligned to the skill sets of the most appropriate candidates. The newly appointed Assistant Heads recognised the need for an intensive programme of training to ensure that they were fully equipped to undertake their roles. Rather than rely on the laissez-faire model that had served well in the past, targets were drawn up and reviews were completed which provided essential information on the effectiveness of the new system. A year later an inspection report of the school was highly complementary about the effectiveness of senior management.

Although most of what is referred to as *Taylorism* isn't considered to be acceptable in modern management parlance, Taylor's ideas do have some support and may be appropriate for the right reason in the right situation with the right people.

Here's a case study based on a contemporary of Taylor's, A. S. Neill, that shows a different approach to management.

CASE STUDY

David was considered an outstanding music teacher. He had been recruited as deputy head of an independent school that used performing arts as a medium for attracting 15/16 year olds who were at risk of exclusion in what were being considered as failing schools. This was a bold move by David who had been in his comfort zone for a number of years but had also recognised that waiting for promotion in his previous school was like waiting for a dead man's shoes.

David had read about A. S. Neill's (1960) work as a headteacher at Summerhill at the beginning of the last century. Neill's approach, where he put his pupils' personal developmental needs before academic achievement, meant that although exam performance results were low, a much higher proportion of pupils found work after leaving school.

David felt that his new role offered him the opportunity to emulate Neill some hundred years after Summerhill was first thought of. Unfortunately, although you could sense the morale of both staff and learners had improved during David's year there, performance figures hadn't.

Dave realised that he wasn't best suited to his new role, when his Head resigned after a heated discussion with the governors over performance. He turned down the role of temporary Head to revert to what he felt he was more comfortable at doing: teaching.

So far we have presented management theory as something where managers are in control, able to take into account all aspects of the current situation and act on those aspects that are key to the situation at hand. If only life was that simple. Very often, managers find themselves having to deal with the swampy lowland messes that occur as a result of the idiosyncratic and unpredictable nature of the people they are managing. **Jon Ronson** (2011) has written an interesting (and amusing) book in which he describes the psychopathic tendencies of people you will meet in the workplace.

It was **Robert Hare** (2003) who developed the Psychopathy Checklist (PCL) as a means of diagnosing psychopathic traits in individuals for clinical, legal or research purposes. Ronson's interpretation of Hare's work offers a more light-hearted perspective. Here is a summary of how we have adapted Hare's theory, using our own headings, to show how the key traits could be found in the people that you are managing:

- The **Seducer**: Charming you and others in a glib and superficial manner.
- The **Ego-maniac**: Having an exaggeratedly high estimation of their ability and refusing to accept criticism.
- The **Procrastinator**: Always coming up with excuses for not meeting set objectives.
- The **Deflector**: Failing to accept responsibility for their own actions and seeking to blame others.

CASE STUDY

Diane thought many of these terms perfectly described the members of her team, though in frequent moments of frustration with the individuals concerned she could also provide a few more colourful ones.

How could she forget the first term in post? One member of her team, Lesley, appeared to lack any drive and the amount of time and effort it needed to motivate her sapped even Diane's much vaunted energy. Another, Mo, was the classic procrastinator, constantly failing to meet deadlines, who also had an unpredictably dangerous mix of the ego-maniac on those occasions when she felt cornered. A third, Norma, was never prepared to accept criticism however justified, looking to pass the blame elsewhere whilst at the same time being only too eager to find fault with others and bring it to the attention of Diane herself. Then there was Paul; always so supportive and encouraging on the surface, but you could not escape the fact that there was a highly personal agenda.

Yet despite the manifestation of such a wide range of traits, Diane concluded there were common themes behind them and that these behaviours were stimulated by any one or a mixture of insecurity and inadequacy or a desire for personal advancement or aggrandisement.

Proposed improvements to homework policy had the potential to trigger the usual battery of behaviour in her team, but an increased awareness of them and the people concerned, whilst not ensuring a smooth transition, helped to obviate the worst excesses. As soon as Paul got wind that there was change in the air, he needed to feel that he was in the vanguard of innovation, collecting points for his CV. Lesley and Mo needed reassurance that the changes were in their own interests, for their negative reactions were the product of a difficulty achieving a work-life balance in the case of Lesley, who had severe family demands, and a real lack of confidence in Mo's case. As for Norma, her antagonism was undiminished and was, as usual, a front for a basic lack of ability. Still you can't win them all. Not all at once anyway, but Diane is still working on it.

Here are six other character traits that you might find amongst the people that you are managing:

- The **Sponge**: Constantly needing to be stimulated.
- The **Shell**: Showing no remorse or guilt if they offend you or others through inappropriate comments.
- The **Unmovable**: Displaying callousness and a lack of empathy with others who may not share their points of view.
- The **Parasite**: Living off the knowledge and skills of their colleagues and falsely claiming credit for ideas.
- The **Results Merchant**: Lacking any drive for long-term development and being obsessed with completing tasks.
- The **Disrupter**: Displaying a tendency to act impulsively and irresponsibly and causing disharmony amongst others they may be working with.

The actual PCL test is administered by trained professionals and done under strict clinical conditions. The model is only used here for illustrative purposes and serves to highlight the extremes in people's behaviours that you may encounter. Should you have to manage people displaying these traits in your organisation, we would advise you to:

- Start by assuming that they will always do the worst thing possible within their trait characteristic.
- Have a strategy in mind for handling the worst possible scenario. If they don't do the worst thing possible, celebrate with a quiet drink and save the strategy for next time. If they do the worst possible thing, keep a clear head and follow the old boxing maxim of defending yourself at all times.
- Implement the planned strategy and keep a record of everything that was said or done. You can still have a quiet drink, but this time to relax.
- Make sure that whatever course of action you take, you follow the rules and regulations set down by your organisation for dealing with people. Even if you were in the right, failure to adhere to correct procedures could result in legal action against you or your organisation.

It's worth making the point here that you will also almost certainly display some of these traits. You need to reflect on this and explore the impact that you have on others.

Hot Tip: Ask yourself: What's making me think the person I am managing has psychopathic traits? Have I got a strategy in place for dealing with them? Am I aware of my own psychopathic traits?

Tony Bush and **David Middlewood** (2006) are two of the most influential contemporary thinkers on educational management. They argue that education provides a unique management challenge because it is geared to the development of human potential. They base this argument on the belief that, if the development of learners is at the heart of the organisation's business, this can only be done effectively if managers in education value the staff who deliver this service. They suggest that if managers want to support staff to flourish they should:

- **Be good role models** by demonstrating a commitment to their own learning and personal and professional development.
- **Support all staff as learners** by recognising that all members of staff are different and have different aspirations both personally and professionally.
- **Encourage the sharing of learning** by developing a network of people who they share knowledge and processes with and act as mentors and mentees with them.

CASE STUDY

Wendy was surprised when her Head, Alan, suggested she become the IT curriculum leader, feeling that she lacked experience and sufficient specialist knowledge of the subject. This was unlike her predecessor, Peter, who had established a local reputation and was on the way to developing a national one too. However, Alan knew that what Wendy lacked in subject expertise she more than made up for in areas that would be far more important in leading and managing a successful department.

For all his expertise in the subject, Peter had struggled to develop new systems of working within the department and often complained to Alan of his frustration with staff because of their failure to implement change at the required pace.

Wendy did not have the baggage of expertise that had made it difficult for Peter to empathise with the problems and shortcomings of staff. Indeed, she herself shared some of these. What Wendy had in abundance was a commitment to self-improvement, which meant honestly and publically admitting her own shortcomings and working hard to redress these. When staff asked for help or advice they quickly learned that they would be dealt with honestly. Wendy was not on an ego trip that made it impossible to say 'I don't know' or 'I didn't think that would happen' (unlike her predecessor), instead opportunities to learn together as a team would be grasped. She was also prepared to take a personal lead, which meant that she was prepared to face the same problems as her staff and on occasions to fail and then react positively by working hard to overcome difficulties.

Although she was no extrovert, in fact she was naturally rather shy and retiring, Wendy was naturally sensitive to team members, aware of their different strengths and weaknesses and conscious that a one-fix-fits-all was not sufficient to get the best out of them. During her time in post Wendy developed a strong, cohesive team who were a strength within the school.

- **Build an emphasis on learning into all management processes** by not getting caught up in the trap of doing things how they've always been done if these are not proving effective.
- **Develop a culture of enquiry and reflection** by not reflecting in isolation and developing communities of reflective practice where enquiry and reflection becomes a shared activity.
- **Assess the effectiveness of staff learning** by having an appreciation of whether or not staff learning policies and practices are proving effective.

Bush and Middlewood claim that valuing and developing staff provides the best prospect of enhanced and sustainable performance by the organisation, but that progress in this direction is likely to be uneven and possibly turbulent. They argue that dealing with this is the ultimate task of management. Here is a member of staff that one of us dealt with during our time as a Head of School.

We've offered the above as examples of how management theory has shifted in emphasis away from the needs of the organisation, with the focus on efficiency gains, to the needs of the individuals, their behaviour patterns and their personal and professional development. But don't get the idea that we think management is all about theory. Practical experience is essential if you want to develop as a manger. You cannot become a great manager by just reading and watching others exercise their skills. You have to jump into the messy lowland swamp that, unfortunately, is often the reality that is management, and get stuck in (not stuck in it).

Management is both an art and a science and anyone can learn the basics. What distinguishes the great from the merely average artist or scientist is their willingness to take risks, to try out new ideas, to fail and to learn from their mistakes. Just reading about management theory is not enough – you have to try out your ideas in practice. You also have to be prepared to fail occasionally.

Hot Tip: There is no disgrace in failure. Remember the only failure you can be criticised for is not trying.

In this chapter we have looked at the distinction between leadership and management. The factor that is common to both is the need to demonstrate professionalism. It's important, however, to draw the distinction between being *a professional* and being *professional*. The former suggests someone who abides by the standards to operate required by licensing authorities (*they do things right*). The latter relates to someone who makes the work-based experience the most valuable one possible for the individual (*they do the right thing*). Inevitably, there has to be a balance between efficiency (*doing things right*) and effectiveness (*doing the right things*), which may be tipped in one way or the other by the financial demands placed on an organisation. This creates a dilemma:

- Being inefficient and failing to satisfy the requirements of the licensing authorities may result in funding being withdrawn from the organisation.
- Being ineffective and failing to satisfy the needs and expectations of its learners may result in learners failing to achieve.

Either way, the organisation becomes vulnerable and may not survive.

The final word on leaders and managers:

- 80 per cent of leadership is inspirational and 20 per cent aspirational.
- 80 per cent of management is aspirational and 20 per cent inspirational.
- Be prepared to look at situations from other people's perspectives and never be afraid to re-examine your own values in light of what they have to say.
- Know what sources of power you have access to and identify who in your organisation exercises power and what you can learn from them.
- Be aware that the day-to-day exchanges, including even the simplest interactions, can have a significant impact on building trust and respect in the organisation.
- Don't think that that you should be deceitful or ruthless in what you do as a leader, but you should be able to play the game in the best interests of your staff and learners.
- Adapt your style of leadership to suit the environment and circumstances you are in.
- Have a strategy in place for dealing with difficult people.
- There is no disgrace in failure: the only failure you can be criticised for is not trying.

2
EQUALITY AND DIVERSITY

The importance of embedding the principles of equality and diversity effectively in the workplace has never been so critical for organisations. The results of the latest census, which show how diverse British society has become in terms of ethnicity, nationality and religion, and the introduction of the Equality Act in 2010 which provides legal protection against discrimination in the workplace in relation to nine characteristics – namely age, disability, gender re-assignment, marriage and civil partnership, pregnancy and maternity, race, religion or belief, sex and sexual orientation – are evidence of this.

Professors **Savita Kumra** and **Simonetta Manfredi** (2012) cover a number of key equality and diversity issues from both a theoretical and practitioner perspective and attempt to marry the two. They claim that:

- The focus in managing work–life balance has shifted from work–family issues to a more inclusive idea of work–life balance to help all workers combine paid work with personal life.
- The implications for employment practices of religious rights of workers have been highlighted by the 2013 decision of the European Court of Human Rights regarding the wearing of a crucifix at work. This has generated significant debate

and interest on the freedom of religion as well as freedom from non-religion in the workplace.

■ The introduction of protection against age discrimination is part of a wider strategy to extend working lives. This has been introduced partly by the result of demographic changes resulting from the combination of a lower birth rate and an ageing population which is placing economic pressure on governments' social security systems and pension funds.

■ Although research has indicated that there is a significant increase in the number of women embarking on professional careers, there is no comparative increase in the numbers of women reaching management or executive positions in their chosen profession.

■ There are misconceptions about the numbers of immigrants entering the UK and also the lack of contribution they make to society. What is becoming clear as the 'facts' are presented is that rather than being a drain on society, immigration is contributing significantly to the vibrancy of life in the UK and overwhelmingly positively in respect of economic contribution.

Kumra and Manfredi argue that their perspectives on equality and diversity constitute debates that leaders will need to engage with in order to align their staffing needs with what is available. To do this:

■ Consider how flexible working arrangements can be used to meet the challenge of integrating workplace-led flexibility with staff-led flexibility. For example look at how allowing classroom support staff to job share might attract experienced staff back into the profession.

■ Make sure that you respond to the challenge of balancing the need to allow religious practices in the organisation with individuals' rights for freedom from the religious interests of other staff and learners.

■ Aim to create a workplace where age becomes irrelevant and the focus is placed entirely on staff members' competencies and abilities.

■ Examine the workplace practices that exist in your organisation that may be preventing the recruitment of, and progression routes for, applicants from under-represented sections of the community. This is particularly acute in primary education where there is a shortage of male teachers.

■ Don't make assumptions about people based on superficial ideas of their perceived membership of any ethnic or disablement group or try to address issues resulting from this by holding short awareness training sessions for staff.

Failing to address any of the above issues will result in prosecution for not complying with the laws of the day, bad public relations and loss of credibility with the statutory authorities.

CASE STUDY

Vera was close to retirement. She had worked for fifteen years as a full-time classroom assistant in the primary section of a special educational needs school. In the run-up to retirement, she asked if it was possible to convert to working part-time. Her daughter and grandchildren lived overseas and working Monday to Wednesday would enable her make frequent trips across to see her family.

Although she made this initial enquiry around Easter time it wasn't until the final week of the school year that she was informed that she would be returning next year on a three-day contract (Wednesday to Friday) to work in the secondary section of the school. Vera had no experience of working in secondary and the days offered meant that she wouldn't be able to get flights to see her family.

When Vera asked to stay in her current role, she was told by her headteacher that her enquiry had been interpreted as a request and plans to reorganise had already been implemented. Furthermore, she told Vera that someone younger with more career ambitions was being allocated the primary role and she could only work Monday to Wednesday. Vera's new role was to accommodate this.

With little or no time to question the decision, Vera had to reluctantly accept the decision. Even offers by a number of Vera's colleagues to change their hours to suit hers were ignored. This caused a lot of ill feeling throughout the school, as Vera was a well-liked and respected member of the school.

Vera did eventually complain to her HR department but little notice was taken of her complaint. When she did retire the following year, her headteacher asked her deputy to officiate at Vera's leaving assembly and didn't even acknowledge Vera as she passed her in the corridor.

Vera's headteacher was lucky in that Vera chose not to rock the boat. Had she decided to make an official complaint, the Head could have been facing serious charges of age discrimination. As it was her actions did very little for the morale of staff in the school.

Hot Tip: Question how clear is your own commitment to this issue.

Rajvinder Kandola and **Johanna Fullerton** (2003) argue that the fundamental principles underpinning managing diversity are acceptance and respect. This requires an understanding that each individual is unique, and respecting individual differences.

These differences can be related to disabilities, ethnicity, gender, race, religious or political beliefs, sexual orientation or socioeconomic status. It is about the exploration of these differences in a safe, positive and supportive environment, and moving beyond simple tolerance to embracing and celebrating the rich dimensions of diversity contained within your workforce.

Kandola and Fullerton liken this situation to a mosaic in which the organisation is made up of a number of pieces of glass, each with their own unique individuality and identity. The analogy with the mosaic is that each individual piece is acknowledged, accepted and has a place in the whole structure.

Managing the MOSAIC effectively is based on the mission statement:

- **M**anagement commitment to developing an ....
- **O**rganisational vision of the workforce of the future and ....
- **S**haring the ownership of the vision with all key stakeholders ....
- **A**ssessing and responding to the needs of everyone through ....
- **I**ndividual focusing and effective ....
- **C**ommunication.

Kandola and Fullerton stress the importance of conducting an audit of needs in an organisation that may identify sources of potential bias and ways in which the culture of the organisation, its structure and processes can overtly or covertly discriminate against individuals.

They further argue that efforts to address discrimination through short awareness training run the risk of not only ingraining stereotypes even further but also of creating new, more powerful stereotypes that simply replace the old ones.

CASE STUDY

A school ran a series of events to highlight the special qualities of Moslems. Asian food was served in the canteen and information on the 'Beauty of the Moslem Faith' was issued to all staff. Rather than participate in the events, some Moslems found this approach to be patronising and offensive and boycotted the events.

Wishing to learn from their mistakes the staff met to consider how they could have done better. They concluded that they had not really identified what they wanted to achieve beyond rather vague notions about raising awareness and enhancing the image of an important group within the community. They also realised that they had missed an important trick in not consulting representatives of the very group on whom they were focusing.

Diversity management is a process intended to create and maintain a positive work environment where the similarities and differences of individuals are valued, so that all can reach their potential and maximise their contributions to an organisation's strategic goals and objectives. To do this effectively:

- Have a clear vision of what you intend to achieve in respect of managing diversity and why this is important.
- Make sure that you have a commitment to being visible, active and ongoing in promoting the vision.
- Play a major role in motivating your staff to focus their energy on working towards the organisational vision.
- Ensure that all initiatives that involve managing diversity are initiated, coordinated and monitored.
- Provide adequate resources to support this.
- Deal with any opposition to the vision. There may be some concern from marginalised groups that the vision will result in a loss of focus and commitment towards their own group's interests.
- Don't try to address opposition to managing diversity by holding short staff training sessions.

Managing diversity has a great deal to offer organisations in recruiting, retaining and getting the best from all their workforce by not making assumptions about people based on superficial ideas of their perceived membership of any group.

> **Hot Tip:** Ask yourself: Am I able to express my vision with clarity and conviction? Can this be articulated in a mission statement that everyone will sign up to?

The final word on equality and diversity:

- Consider how flexible working arrangements can be used to meet the challenge of integrating workplace-led flexibility with staff-led flexibility.
- Make sure that you respond to the challenge of balancing the need to allow religious practices in the organisation with individuals' rights for freedom from the religious interests of other staff and learners.
- Aim to create a workplace where age becomes irrelevant and the focus is placed entirely on staff members' competencies and abilities.
- Don't make assumptions about people based on superficial ideas of their perceived membership of any ethnic or disablement group.
- Question how clear is your own commitment to this issue.
- Ask yourself: Am I able to express my vision for equality and diversity with clarity and conviction?
- Can this vision be articulated in a mission statement that everyone will sign up to?

3

SAFEGUARDING

Childhood abuse is any act of aggression or omission by an adult that results in harm, potential for harm or threat of harm to a child. It can occur in the child's home, school or any community setting the child attends.

The different forms of abuse include:

Physical abuse: This involves non-accidental physical injury to a child.

Neglect: This involves the failure of the child's parent or caregiver to provide for physiological needs such as food, warmth and shelter.

Emotional maltreatment: This involves the constant belittling or rejection of a child by someone considered close to them.

Sexual abuse/exploitation: This involves any act where an adult abuses a child for sexual gratification.

According to the 2016 report from the National Society for the Prevention of Cruelty to Children (Bentley et al., 2016):

- There are currently over 50,000 children in the UK who are identified as needing protection from abuse.
- This represents just 12.5 per cent of the number of children who are being abused.

- One in twenty children in the UK have been sexually abused.
- One in three children who were sexually abused did not report the abuse.
- Over 90 per cent of children who were abused were abused by someone they knew.
- Nearly 3,000 children were identified as needing protection from sexual abuse in 2014.

The safeguarding of children and vulnerable adults is at the heart of any civilised society. The UK has built upon a system of disclosure and barring checks and a raft of policy guidance to develop processes that ensure that those working with children and vulnerable adults are appropriate to do so. This section explores the implications of this to education and the roles of safeguarding leaders. Although the emphasis is on safeguarding children, the principles apply equally well to vulnerable adults.

In September 2016, the Department for Education launched its statutory guidance for schools and colleges *Keeping Children Safe in Education*. The document contained information on what schools and colleges should do and set out the legal duties with which schools and colleges must do in order to comply with legislation to keep children (defined as under the age of 18) safe.

The guidance stressed that everyone who comes into contact with children and their families and carers has a role to play in safeguarding children. In order to fulfil this responsibility effectively, all educational leaders should make sure their organisation's approach is to consider, at all times, what is in the best interests of the child. This involves 'protecting children from maltreatment; preventing impairment of children's health or development; ensuring that children grow up in circumstances consistent with the provision of safe and effective care; and taking action to enable all children to have the best outcomes'.

Here are some key points, taken from the guidance, which you need to be aware of in order to ensure that all staff members fulfill their obligations to safeguard the welfare of the children in their care. They are that all staff members should:

- Be aware of systems within their school or college which support safeguarding and these should be explained to them as part of staff induction. This should include: the child protection policy and the staff behaviour policy (sometimes called a code of conduct).
- Receive appropriate safeguarding and child protection training which is regularly updated. In addition all staff members should receive safeguarding and child protection updates (e.g. via email, e-bulletins and staff meetings) as required, but at least annually, to provide them with the relevant skills and knowledge to safeguard children effectively.
- Be aware of the early help process, and understand their role in it. This includes identifying emerging problems, liaising with the designated safeguarding lead,

sharing information with other professionals to support early identification and assessment and, in some cases, acting as the lead professional in undertaking an early help assessment.

- Be aware of the process for making referrals to children's social care and for statutory assessments under the Children Act 1989 that may follow a referral, along with the role they might be expected to play in such assessments.
- Know what to do if a child tells them he/she is being abused or neglected. Staff should know how to manage the requirement to maintain an appropriate level of confidentiality whilst at the same time liaising with relevant professionals such as the designated safeguarding lead and children's social care.
- Never promise a child that they will not tell anyone about an allegation, as this may ultimately not be in the best interests of the child.
- Be aware of the types of abuse and neglect so that they are able to identify cases of children who may be in need of help or protection.

Although safeguarding the welfare of children is the role of everyone in the organisation, most schools and colleges will have a designated safeguarding leader who will take on the responsibilities for:

- Discussing with any staff members who have expressed concerns about a child and agreeing what action to take.
- Ensuring that they are kept in touch about any direct referrals made by staff members who feel a child is in immediate danger.
- Documenting any concerns and any action taken and following up on this.
- Pressing for reconsideration if the child's situation does not appear to be improving to ensure that their concerns have been addressed and, most importantly, that the child's situation improves.
- Supporting the staff member in liaising with other agencies and setting up an inter-agency assessment as appropriate.
- Keeping the case under constant review and giving consideration to a referral to children's social care if the child's situation does not appear to be improving.

One of the sad aspects of children who are being abused is that they feel they have done something wrong and that they are to blame. They often find silence is the only way to survive.

Safeguarding leaders have a major role to play in supporting staff to deal effectively with children who may not have either the experience or maturity to unravel the inner turmoil they face at being abused. By encouraging teaching staff to adopt a caring attitude and a willingness to listen, teachers will provide a trusting environment in which the child will begin to recognise that they are capable and valued.

CASE STUDY

Brian was nine years old and was on an overnight field trip when he was first sexually abused by someone who was a respected teacher, member of the church and family friend. The abuse continued after the trip with Brian and some friends being lured into the classroom storeroom for the abuser's gratification. Brian describes the fact that the physical response was not one of repulsion and that he thought he was just being naughty as causing him the greatest shame. He attributes these feelings of shame and not wanting to hurt his parents as the reasons why he kept quiet for so long about the abuse.

Brian grew up to be a successful solicitor, charismatic member of the England Grand Slam winning rugby team in the 1990s and television commentator. Few people who have ever seen Brian Moore (aka 'Pitbull') play rugby, and his aggressive and uncompromising style of play, would have associated him with the same man whose upsetting and heart-rendering interview about the effects of his abuse on BBC news in 2013 helped to highlight the devastating effect that childhood abuse has on people.

Hot Tip: Ask yourself: Is everyone with a stake in the school aware of systems within the school which support safeguarding?

PREVENTING EXTREMISM

Extremism can take many forms, including political, religious and misogynistic extremism. Protecting children from any extremist views they may encounter, now or later in their lives, is arguably one of the most challenging issue facing leaders in education today.

The Department for Education's 2015(c) guide to schools and childcare providers, *The Prevent Duty*, explains what the duty means for schools and childcare providers. The guidance makes it clear what they should do to demonstrate compliance with the duty and informs them about other sources of information, advice and support. It does not stipulate that they need to have a dedicated Prevent policy. They should, however, have clear procedures in place for protecting children at risk of radicalisation which may be set out in their existing safeguarding policies.

The following may, but not exclusively, indicate that a student could be in danger of or undergoing the process of radicalisation:

- Possessing and distributing extremist literature.
- Using extremist ideology to explain their personal disadvantage.
- Justifying the use of violence to solve societal issues.
- Boasting of joining extremist groups.
- Significant changes in their appearance and/or behaviour.

Most teachers are encouraged to undertake the same method of making a referral as they would if they had concerns regarding a safeguarding issue. The 5-Rs is a standard method of doing this:

- **Recognise**: Ask what signs of radicalisation are evident.
- **React**: Listen in to conversations between parties. Don't interfere. Don't ask leading questions.
- **Record**: Immediately record the detail of what you saw, overheard or witnessed.
- **Report**: Pass on the details immediately to the appropriate personnel. Do you know who they are?
- **Reflect**: Take time to reflect on the outcome of what happened. Ask yourself if it could have been handled differently.

CASE STUDY

The 'Trojan horse' controversy which rocked Birmingham schools in 2014 was sparked by an anonymous letter outlining a plot called to oust headteachers and replace them with people who would run schools on strict Islamic lines.

Ian Kershaw (Adams, 2014), an independent education expert commissioned by Birmingham City Council to investigate the allegations, reported that there was no evidence of a systematic plot to take over schools or of a conspiracy to promote 'an anti-British agenda through violent extremism or radicalisation in schools in East Birmingham'. Kershaw further concluded that the people involved seemed to be motivated by a 'genuine and understandable desire' to 'raise standards' but that hardline governors in some Birmingham schools were guilty of 'serious malpractice' and that Headteachers were being undermined in order to introduce Islamic worship and ban sex education. The report added that the hardline governors – mainly men of Pakistani heritage – used 'inappropriate, unprofessional and disruptive behaviour' and were 'overly challenging and sometimes aggressive' towards Headteachers who resisted their proposals.

The report indicated that a number of schools in East Birmingham had introduced Islamic assemblies without permission and used the Muslim call to prayer which had 'led to the coercion of young people' to participate in worship during the school day.

The report concluded by claiming that the problem had been compounded by the failure of Birmingham City Council to challenge the governors and support the Headteachers for fear of being accused of being racist or Islamophobic.

Having policies and procedures in place to prevent extremism is important for leaders but they often fail to capture the hearts and minds of children. Here is an approach developed by a theatre group, The Play House, in the West Midlands, that attempts to do just that.

Tapestry is an interactive theatre performance and workshop programme originally designed and developed by The Play House in partnership with the West Midlands Counter Terrorist Unit (CTU) and Birmingham City Council (BCC) as part of the Prevent programme in 2009 to challenge extremist ideology, as well as providing tools for participants to challenge it in a real situation. Here is a summary of what *Tapestry* is about:

An opening montage of very short scenes was developed to illustrate the current context to the drama, making references to a range of incidents and issues, including 'lone wolf' Anders Brevik, ISIS, young people leaving the UK to fight in Syria, the beheading of charity worker Alan Hemming, and social media being used as a tool by extremists such as *Britain First*'s technique of using popular and inoffensive-seeming posts on Facebook that click through to a right-wing extremist political organisation.

The performance is introduced by the narrator, who explains the format of the session. A brief exercise is conducted to assess participants' attitudes by asking them to give a thumbs up or a thumbs down to indicate whether they agree with three statements: 'There is more that unites us than divides us'; 'I am allowed to say whatever I want, even if it offends you'; and 'If you want things to change, you have to be prepared to fight'.

For the drama, the three main characters are: Hassan, a young Muslim man of Pakistani heritage; Jason, a young white man; and Naz, a mixed-race Muslim woman who knows them both. The performers have researched and prepared a back story for each of their characters so that they can refer to these during the hot-seating that follows the drama. This is where children are allowed to question each of the characters' behaviour.

Projects such as *Tapestry*, which focus on both extreme right-wing and Al Qaida inspired ideology, provide participants with the opportunity to discuss the issues outlined in a fictional context that has been carefully constructed to ensure that they are able to express their views freely and challenge the views of others in a safe environment. Whilst contact with individual children is limited because their engagement is through a one-off session, its format means that the project can reach large numbers over a short space of time, addressing several different outcomes of the Prevent strategy.

Hot Tip: Ask yourself: Are we doing more than just issuing policy statements to capture the hearts and minds of people on this issue?

The final word on safeguarding:

- All stakeholders in the school should be aware of the policies and practices relating to safeguarding.
- All staff should receive appropriate safeguarding and child protection training which is regularly updated.
- All staff should aware of the early help process, and understand their role in it.
- All staff should be aware of the process for making referrals to children's social care.
- All staff should know what to do if a child tells them he/she is being abused or neglected.
- All staff should know how to manage the requirement to maintain an appropriate level of confidentiality whilst at the same time liaising with relevant professionals.
- No member of staff should ever promise a child that they will not tell anyone about an allegation, as this may ultimately not be in the best interests of the child.
- Staff should be aware of the types of abuse and neglect so that they are able to identify cases of children who may be in need of help or protection.
- Ask yourself: Are we doing more than just issuing policy statements to capture the hearts and minds of people on this issue?

4

COACHING AND MENTORING

As a leader or manager in any organisation you have a tough job. In an educational context this becomes even more problematic because you are dealing almost exclusively with people rather than products. You are probably under intense pressure to improve learner performance results, often with too few resources in terms of time and money. We suspect that this has always been the case, but never more so than in the present day with a pace of change that's bewildering and a level of expectation that's fierce. You have one key asset that makes your task less daunting and that's your people. Nothing will allow you to achieve more than having a skilled and motivated team working for you.

The ability to raise the performance of your staff is an important element of being a good leader or manager. Through effective coaching and mentoring you can develop the people around you to be more skilled in necessary areas and to take on more responsibility, thus freeing yourself up to deal with the other aspects of school leadership such as strategic planning and budgeting. It's important, however, to make the point at the very beginning of this chapter that both good coaching and mentoring are skills that require a depth of understanding and plenty of practice if you want them to pay dividends for you, your organisation and your staff. Sadly, the converse is true and those who go through the motions of coaching or mentoring fail to achieve the intended results.

It's important to locate coaching and mentoring in respect of the various human resource development approaches that can take place in an organisation. A good starting point is to use the metaphor of *learning to drive*:

- A *consultant* will advise you on the most appropriate car to drive.
- A *counsellor* will try to address any anxieties that you have about driving.
- A *mentor* will share their own driving experiences with you.
- A *coach* will encourage you to get in and drive the car correctly.

The measures can be represented in terms of the 'challenging and supporting' and 'directive and non-directive' approaches shown in Figure 4.1.

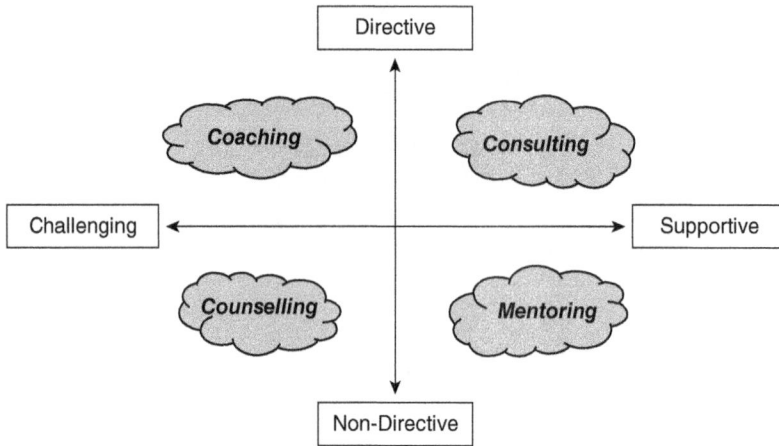

Figure 4.1   The intervention model

The one thing that unites each of the above approaches is that they seek some form of behaviour modification in either the organisation or the individual member of staff. Think of this in terms of the *desired state* to describe the outcome required. If you are teaching someone to drive, the *desired state* is that they can get from A to B effectively and efficiently. We prefer to use this term because the use of *state* infers movement from one position to another and *desire* as the motivation to get there.

If the purpose of the coach or mentor is to support the person to move towards their desired state, then it's understandable that you might think that coaching and mentoring are the same thing. It's important therefore that we discuss the differences in each of the approaches in terms of relationships, time, structure and outcome:

- Coaches are usually experienced professionals who work with people on developing specific skills. Mentors are usually experienced individuals who share knowledge and experiences with a less experienced person.
- Coaching can be as short as a single session or part of a session that may be necessary for the person to develop understanding or a particular skill. Mentoring requires time to develop a relationship of mutual trust in which both partners can learn about one another and feel safe in sharing the real issues that the person is facing.

- Coaches set the topic, the pace and the learning methods to help develop skills. Mentors will tailor their approaches to meet the individual's needs.
- Coaching is a task oriented activity with the focus on concrete issues and easy-to-measure performance output. Mentoring is relationship oriented with the focus on mutual development.

John Whitmore (1998) developed the *GROW* model in the early 1980s. He suggests that the model is a simple but powerful way of getting the best out of your staff and can be used by leaders and managers who undertake coaching or mentoring. He likens it to thinking about planning a journey in which you decide where you are going (the **G**oal), establish where you are at present (the **R**eality), explore the various routes (the **O**ptions) and be committed to reaching your destination (the **W**ill to succeed). The various constituents of the model can be summarised as:

Establish the Goal: Look at what the individual wants to achieve and express this in terms of what they will be like when they have achieved it.

Examine the current Reality: Encourage the individual to avoid trying to solve problems before considering where they are at present.

Explore the Options: After exploring the reality, turn the individual's attention to determining what is possible.

Establish the Will: Now that the options are clear, get the individual to commit to specific actions in order to move towards achieving their goal.

Whitmore stresses the importance of the coach or mentor not considering themself to be an expert in the other person's predicament and not trying to solve their problems for them. He describes the ultimate role of the coach and mentor as being a facilitator who helps the person to select the best options.

Using Whitmore's model as the basis for any actions that you take to develop your staff, here is our idea of the continuum from coaching to mentoring via critical friendship.

COACHING

Bob Bates (2015) developed the *COACHING* model after a comprehensive review of 76 theories and models related to coaching. Bates uses the acronym *COACHING* to represent eight key elements that he argues should be present in any coaching programme. Here is a summary of the elements:

Clarify the role: Establish who does what, when, where and how.

Organise goals and objectives: Get the people you are working with to have a vision about what they could be and set goals that will help them to achieve this vision.

Act with conviction: Choose the most appropriate method for coaching an individual/group and see it through with conviction and commitment.

Confirm that expectations are being met: Elicit feedback not just on the outcome but also on the process undertaken, and be prepared to make changes if necessary.

Have a strategy for dealing with setbacks: Accept that bad things happen and deal with them.

Inspire creative thinking: Encourage the person you are coaching to be willing to think outside of the box.

Never be afraid of failure: If the person you are coaching fails at a task, it doesn't mean that you or the individual is a failure; it simply means that they have failed the task.

Get to know the person you are coaching: Build a relationship that is based on respect and trust.

CASE STUDY

Dave was 26, had taught in two primary schools and secured a deputy headship in a large, well-established primary school with a good reputation. The headteacher told Dave that he appointed him as a 'head in training' and from day one coached him to make decisions as if he were head. He told Dave that he could be headteacher any day, if he was ill, moved on or died.

He also made it clear that when he wasn't around (which was frequently) Dave was in sole charge. He told Dave 'You are not minding the shop. I never want to come back to be told there is something to sort out – you have to have sorted it or put into process whatever was needed to resolve it.' Dave thought that this was a steep learning curve.

One of the headteacher's mantras was 'The ultimate delegation is abdication!' and he certainly tried (or perhaps appeared to try) to make himself dispensable. This was his style. This was his belief. His strengths were his coaching abilities, affording professional development opportunities for all staff, a caring attitude, a love of people and, above all, total support for his staff. When Dave asked him about his leadership, he replied, 'I don't know. Sometimes I think I lead from the front and sometimes from the back. I've never thought about it. You'll have to ask everyone.'

He criticised but never blamed, and said on many occasions 'Honest mistakes are our friends we learn from.' Of course, he meant that we learn from errors and we learn from colleagues. When Dave was leaving to take up his first headship, his headteacher gave him one piece of advice: 'If I've ever done something you think worked, copy it but do it better. If I've ever gone wrong, learn, don't copy, and do it your way.'

Bates suggests that the thing that differentiates coaching from other measures is the level of challenge and direction that takes place: challenge in respect of getting people to deliver the desired outcomes; direction in terms of telling them what to do or getting them to think and do it for themselves.

The head in this case study was not afraid to share his skills and knowledge of leadership with his assistant but he made the point that he should not be afraid of making key decisions and never to be afraid of failure; just to make sure that he learned from this.

> **Hot Tip:** Ask yourself if you have the right level of challenge and direction that will achieve the desired outcomes.

CRITICAL FRIENDSHIP

Arthur Costa and **Bena Kallick** (1983) use the concept of *critical friendship* as a variation on the theme of coaching and mentoring. They describe a critical friend as a trusted person who asks provocative questions, provides a different perspective on an issue facing someone and critiques their actions with good intent. They outline a six-phase process for the critical friend–individual interaction that can be summarised as:

Engagement: The individual outlines the problem and asks the critical friend for feedback.

Questioning: The critical friend asks questions in order to understand the root causes of the problem and to clarify the context in which the problem is occurring.

Desired outcomes: The individual sets the desired outcomes for the interaction, thus ensuring they are in control.

Feedback: The critical friend provides feedback on what seems to be significant about the problem. This feedback should be more than a cursory look at the problem and should provide an alternative viewpoint that helps address the problem.

Reflection: Both parties reflect on what was discussed.

Recording: The individual records their views on the points and suggestions raised. The critical friend records the advice given and makes a note of what follow-up action they need to take.

Costa and Kallick argue that the manager as a critical friend is a very powerful idea, perhaps because it contains an inherent tension within the term: friends bring a high degree of unconditional positive regard, whereas critics may be negative and intolerant of failure. They describe the ideal as a marriage of unconditional support and unconditional critique.

CASE STUDY

Tim was the principal of a federation of three schools, each with a Head of School. He felt that the strength of the federation's senior leadership team would be undermined if he were responsible for the formal performance management of the heads of the schools and therefore bought in expertise from Barbara, an educational consultant with years of experience in the field, to undertake this. The wisdom of this decision was illustrated soon after, when Sally, the head of one of the schools in the federation, experienced difficulty with the attitudes and behaviour of a group of parents on the school site before and after school sessions.

Sally was grateful that Tim had appointed a third party to undertake her formal appraisal because it made her feel more comfortable about enlisting his assistance in sorting out the problem, without any fear of her performance being judged and counting against her in her appraisal. By the same token Tim felt free to act as a critical friend and was able to provide helpful advice in resolving Sally's problem.

Sally was grateful that Tim had acted as he had because it made her feel more comfortable about enlisting his assistance in sorting out the problem, without any fear of her performance being judged. By the same token the Principal felt free to act as a critical friend.

Hot Tip: Ask yourself: Are the boundaries clear to both of us? Am I giving feedback in an honest and critical manner?

MENTORING

In Greek mythology, Mentor was a friend of Odysseus, who gave him the responsibility of looking after his son Telemachus, when he went to fight in the Trojan wars. The word 'mentor' evolved to mean trusted advisor, friend, teacher or wise person. It has become a significant aspect of human development, particularly with learning, where one person invests their time, energy and personal know-how in assisting the growth of their staff.

Chip Bell (2002) devised a questionnaire for the purpose of determining whether or not someone had the qualities to be a good mentor. The questionnaire (obtainable online) is based on a series of 39 questions with two possible answers. The individual is asked to indicate which of the two answers fits them best.

Examples of the questions and responses include:

- People see me as ..... (a) Hard-nosed (b) A Soft-touch
- When it comes to social situations, I ..... (a) Hold back (b) Jump in

- Work days that I like most are ….. (a) Unpredictable (b) Well-planned
- My approach to planning my personal activities is ….. (a) Easy-going (b) Orderly
- I prefer to express myself to others in ways that are ….. (a) Indirect (b) Direct

Bell claims that the responses to these questions measure, at a given moment in time, the mentor's capacity for *sociability, dominance* and *openness*. These can be summarised as:

Sociability: This relates to the mentor's preference for being with or apart from others. People with high sociability scores will find the rapport-building and dialogue-leading dimensions of mentoring easier.

Dominance: This relates to the mentor's preference for being in charge. This is a major issue in mentoring, where the relationship is built on shared power. People with high dominance scores may be reluctant to share control.

Openness: This relates to the mentor's capacity to trust others and to generate their trust in them. People with low openness scores are likely to be cautious, guarded and reluctant to show feelings.

Bell argues that the *Mentor Scale* is not there to judge or criticise someone as a person but rather to help evaluate their strengths and areas for development and to tease out any blind spots they have in terms of their ability to be a mentor.
    Here are some tips to helping you become a better mentor:

- Take time getting to know one another. Draw up a picture of the person that you are mentoring with through meaningful conversation. Establish rapport and identify areas of mutual interest.
- Discuss the purpose of the interaction. Find out what previous experience they have had of being mentored. Share some of your own experiences of mentoring or being mentored. This will demonstrate that you are able to understand and empathise with their feelings.
- Determine the individual's goals and what they want to get out of the relationship. Be absolutely sure about what they need from you.
- Describe what you feel you can and can't do. Don't build up a level of expectation of support that you can't provide.
- Share your assumptions, needs and limitations candidly.
- Discuss what opportunities and options exist and the most useful kind of assistance you can provide.

Telling the person that you are mentoring what to do may not be the best thing for them. Supporting them to decide for themself will give them ownership of the issue.

CASE STUDY

One of us was once asked to be the mentor for a student teacher completing her Certificate in Education training. We set down the ground rules that she was in charge of determining the frequency of our meetings, what the agenda for each meeting would be and what contribution she expected from her mentor.

In the two years it took her to complete her Cert Ed, she never logged one mentor meeting with us. When she invited us to her graduation ceremony, we asked her why she wanted us there as we'd done nothing to help her. She told us that on the contrary, the fact that she knew we were there to support her if anything went wrong had been a great help.

Hot Tip: Take time to get to know the person you are mentoring. Find out what the mentee wants out of your mentoring. Be honest in what you feel you can, or can't, achieve with your mentee.

An interesting corollary to Bell's mentor scale is that if you score low on the mentor scale, you may actually be more suited to being a coach.

The final word on coaching and mentoring:

- Coaches are usually experienced professionals who work with people on developing specific skills. They set the topic, the pace and the learning methods to help develop skills.
- Coaching is a task-oriented activity with the focus on concrete issues and easy-to-measure performance output.
- Coaching can be as short as a single session or part of a session that may be necessary for the person to develop understanding or a particular skill.
- Ask yourself if you have the right level of challenge and direction to be a coach that will achieve the desired outcomes.
- Mentors are usually experienced individuals who share knowledge and experiences with a less experienced person. They will tailor their approaches to meet the individual's needs.
- Mentoring is relationship-oriented with the focus on mutual development.
- Mentoring requires time to develop a relationship of mutual trust in which both partners can learn about one another and feel safe in sharing the real issues that the person is facing.

- A critical friend is a trusted person who asks provocative questions, provides a different perspective on an issue facing someone and critiques their actions with good intent.
- Take time to get to know the person you are supporting.
- Find out what the individual wants out of your support.
- Be honest in what you feel you can, or can't, achieve with the individual you are supporting.
- Make sure that the coaching/mentoring boundaries are clear to both you and the person you are working with.
- Be certain that you are giving and receiving feedback in an honest and critical manner.

5
TEAMS

We are not, by nature, good team members. Watch a pack of wolves in one of David Attenborough's wonderful wildlife series isolate a weaker member of a herd of buffalos and move in for the kill and you may think that we could learn much about how other animals work as a team. See the same pack fight viciously over a small morsel of food and you may think otherwise. Before we get hate mail, we're not suggesting that people who work in education bear any resemblance to a pack of wolves!

In order for people to find a reason to work as members of a team, however, they do need a common purpose and a sense of identity. Put a group of people in a lift together and they will think and act as individuals. Create a crisis situation (a breakdown or fire) and the need for survival will become the common purpose, with each individual assuming a role (comforter, problem solver etc.). In education, the crisis may be something threatening like a downturn in data trend, or the redrafting of the curriculum or assessment procedures, or something less-threatening but nonetheless challenging like organising an after-school club or school concert.

Having the right team members, meticulous planning and clarity of vision are arguably the most critical aspect of effective educational leadership and management. Let's have a look at three cases in question, all taken from the world of sport.

CASE STUDY: *They think it's all over*

We can't believe that it is over fifty years since England's only success in the soccer world cup. In the 1966 World Cup Final, Alf Ramsey took the unpopular decision to leave out his star striker for the final against West Germany. Instead he picked Geoff Hurst, whose style better suited his team plan. Hurst scored the only ever hat-trick in a World Cup Final and England became World Champions.

Ramsey's success rested on a dubious decision by a Russian linesman who was adamant that a shot from Hurst had crossed the line for a goal. The whole of West Germany (it was a divided country then) were equally adamant that it hadn't, and even modern technology has failed to resolve the dispute. On such fine decisions are reputations of great leadership (Ramsey was knighted for his achievement) made or broken.

Before we leave the Ramsey story we want to make one thing clear: building and managing teams is difficult and even the best managers can get it wrong sometimes. Four years later, in Mexico, Sir Alf made the catastrophic decision to substitute his best player and talisman, Bobby Charlton, when England were beating West Germany 2–0 in the quarter finals. Ramsey wanted to rest Charlton for a crucial semi-final game. With Charlton gone, West Germany stormed back into the game and ended up winning 3–2. If it can happen to Alf Ramsey at the height of his career, it can happen to you. If it does, don't be too hard on yourself. Learn from your mistakes and move on. After all, it's not as if someone will still be talking about your failure forty odd years from now.

CASE STUDY: *Failing to prepare is preparing to fail*

Another remarkable example of teambuilding and subsequent success in recent years was England's victory in the 2003 Rugby World Cup. The Head Coach, Clive Woodward, attributed England's success not just to an outstanding group of players, but also to having the most intensive preparation of any international team and a powerful team spirit both on and off the pitch. He paid particular tribute to the roles filled with precision and passion by the many players and backroom staff that made up the team.

Unfortunately, after his great team of 2003 disbanded, Woodward never reached the same heights, and after a disastrous tour as the coach of the 2005 British Lions' tour to New Zealand, when the Lions were hammered in all three test matches, Woodward retired from coaching rugby to concentrate on a career in soccer administration.

Never one to ascribe to the belief that the battle of Waterloo was won on the playing fields of Eton, a reference to where great leaders came from, here is a case study that doesn't involve success in a ball sport and would be more at home in the Manchester Velodrome than Eton.

CASE STUDY: *It's the little things that count*

Many of you will know of household names such as Chris Hoy and Bradley Wiggins. Both were knighted as a result of their services to the sport of cycling. Fewer will know about another cycling knight, David Brailsford, the coach behind the successes of British cyclists over the past five years. Brailsford attributed these successes to his meticulous approach to planning.

This started with his audacious mission to win a pot full of world championship and Olympic gold medals and to do what no other British rider had come anywhere near to doing: winning the Tour de France. His aim was to do this within five years; he achieved it in three. He set challenging objectives and relentlessly pursued the tiniest gains in everything - the bikes, the riders' fitness levels, their clothing, nutrition and teamwork. He referred to this as the *aggregation of marginal gains*. His attention to measuring these gains was evident when Wiggins crossed the line to become the first ever British winner of the Tour de France: he made sure that he punched the button on his data clock before punching the air with joy.

In this chapter so far, we have looked at the role that team leaders play in leading teams to success (or failure, as subsequent to their great successes all three came down to earth with a bit of a bump). We now want to look at the roles that people play within teams and the factors that may affect their capacity to perform at high levels within the team. We have drawn on some really great classical theories relating to the subject from people such as George Homans, Meredith Belbin, Bruce Tuckman and Susan Wheelan that will help you to understand the factors that influence your

---

Charles Handy (1993) tells a good story of how he once described ineffective teams as being like a rowing eight: 'eight people going backwards without talking to one another, being guided by someone who was too small to see where they were going'. He got a bit of flak from an oarsman in the audience who argued that they were 'The perfect team: as they would not have the confidence to pull on the oar so strongly without talking or seeing if they did not have complete trust in each other and in the little person at the rudder'.

team selection and development. We've also taken a break from the world of sport with a trip to the cinema and some really classic movies to use as case studies. Before this, a few words of wisdom from one of the UK's most influential thinkers on management for our final sporting reference in this chapter:

Of course, we all want our team to do more than what's expected of them but it's also important to be alert to the potential differences between how you expect the team to act outwardly and their natural way of behaving. This can be a source of tension within the team and certain team members may rebel against this by developing their own informal rules. You may consider that this will be healthy for team dynamics but, if you let it get out of hand, you could be facing a revolt.

George Homans (1958) argues that the characteristic of every team is influenced by the environment in which it functions. He claims that, as a result of this, the interaction between the team and the environment will shape the behaviour of the team and the final outcome. There are five elements that determine this relationship:

Physical: The physical restraints imposed on the team that affect its performance.

Cultural–personal: The beliefs and values that make up the shared understanding of the team.

Technological: The facilities and resources the team have at their disposal to support their activities.

Organisational: The organisation's policies and procedures that govern the working practices and personal development of the team.

Socio-economical: The impact that the wider political, economical, social and technological developments have on the team's work.

Homans argues that, influenced by the environment, the group go through a stage of behaving in a manner expected by the group leader (required or given behaviours) through a stage of doing things over and above what was expected (emergent behaviours), resulting ultimately in increased productivity and personal development.

Let's take our first trip to the cinema and the 1993 film *Gettysburg* to see Homan's ideas in practice:

Based on true events, the film *Gettysburg* depicts one of the major events of the American Civil War: the Battle of Gettysburg. Joshua Chamberlain (played by Jeff Daniels) is a northern general holding a defensive position during the battle. At a crucial moment in the confrontation, he goes against all the conventions of warfare, and direct orders from his commander in chief, by attacking an overwhelming opposing force rather than defending the position. His actions turned the battle, won the war, and the rest is history.

Great! Chamberlain's actions worked but, what are the implications of regular diso-bedience by members of the team? Give them enough latitude but remember where the buck stops.

You may not be doing anything as serious as fighting for the abolition of slavery, but you still have to get things done. Have a good look at what you have within the team in terms of the skill mix, the resources and whether their behaviour is suitable for the task.

> **Hot Tip:** Look at the wider social, environmental and economic factors that will affect a team's performance.

SELECTING THE TEAM MEMBERS

One way of looking at the skill mix in the team is to look at the theories of **Meredith Belbin** (1981). The principles that underpin Belbin's work are simple: in order for teams to be successful, certain functions or roles must be undertaken. He suggests that the following roles must be filled for well-balanced teamworking to exist:

Coordinator: Sets the agenda for team meetings, clarifies the team's objectives, establishes priorities and facilitates discussion.

Completer finisher: Has a key role to play towards the end of a task when people are flagging and work needs polishing.

Team worker: Helps to settle issues (personal as well as professional) within the team and helps the team to gel.

Implementer: Turns strategy into action.

Shaper: Drives the team towards its objectives, engenders a sense of urgency and maintains momentum.

Monitor evaluator: Analyses what the team are committing themselves to and measures their progress objectively.

Resource investigator: Finds the resources necessary to achieve the team's objectives.

Plant: Comes up with original ideas on how to approach tasks in the team.

Specialist: Provides the team with technical expertise in key areas.

Belbin acknowledges that people may be expected to fill more than one role in the team, especially in the smaller teams that are characteristic of schools, and that the duplication of certain roles can lead to conflict within the team.

It's very rare that you will be given the opportunity to handpick all the members of your team. Therefore you need to be clear about which role/s each person will play. Belbin's Team Roles Questionnaire (available from www.belbin.com) can help you identify team members' preferred roles. Like all psychological question-naires it's not infallible, but it is a useful start. Once you have allocated the roles it is essential to brief each member of the team individually on what you expect from them.

Let's take another trip to the cinema and the 1963 film *The Great Escape* to make a bit more sense of Belbin's ideas:

The Great Escape is a film based on a true story about a special *stalag,* or prison camp, built by the Germans in 1944 to house troublesome prisoners-of-war. With the common purpose of escape, the prisoners begin to work as a team: Squadron Leader Bartlett (played by Richard Attenborough) coordinates activities; Captain Hilts (played by Steve McQueen) proves to be the driving force behind people's desire to escape; Lt. Velinski (played by Charles Bronson) is the expert on tunneling; Lt. 'Scrounger' Hendley (played by James Garner) gets the materials they need to make things work; and Lt. Blythe (played by Donald Pleasance) is responsible for making the forged passports.

It's important that you constantly analyse what's going on within the team and identify both problems and their causes. For example:

- If there's a lack of awareness of where the team is at a given moment and what needs to be done to move the team forward, then ask yourself if you are leading the team correctly.
- If there's a lack of clarity about the team's objectives and how the team will achieve them, and if you are not to blame, then check out your *shaper.*
- If there's an inability to come up with new ideas, ask yourself what the team *plant* is doing.
- If the team is underperforming, ask yourself how good your *monitor evaluator* is.
- If the team is encountering difficulties in turning ideas into practical solutions, find out what your *implementer* is doing.
- If there's a lack of resources, see if you can swop your *resource investigator* for someone with a bit more ingenuity.
- If there's a lack of harmony within the team, find out what the *team worker* is doing.
- If there's an inability to finish tasks off, question if your team's *completer finisher* has become bored with the project.
- If a lack of specialist knowledge is slowing the project down, ask yourself if your *specialist* has the right expertise/knowledge for this team.

By the way, please don't be deterred from using this approach just because most of the escapees in the film were caught and shot!

> **Hot Tip:** Make sure that you have the right people in the right roles in your project team.

As the team leader it's important that you are aware of where the team is at any given moment and what needs to be done to move it forward. Therefore you need to constantly analyse what is going on and identify both problems and their cause. Once you have identified a problem within the team you have to deal with it. Tackling poor performance is not easy. In the final analysis you may have to expel an existing member from the team. This is never pleasant, but as team leader you must remember that no individual is above the team. One way of avoiding this unpleasantness is to focus on the development of the team and one of the really great teamworking theories.

DEVELOPING THE TEAM

Bruce Tuckman (1965) first presented his classic Forming, Storming, Norming, Performing (FSNP) model in 1965 and, with Mary Jensen, added a fifth stage (Adjourning) in 1977. The model describes the phases which teams tend to go through from initial formation through to completion of the task (see Figure 5.1).

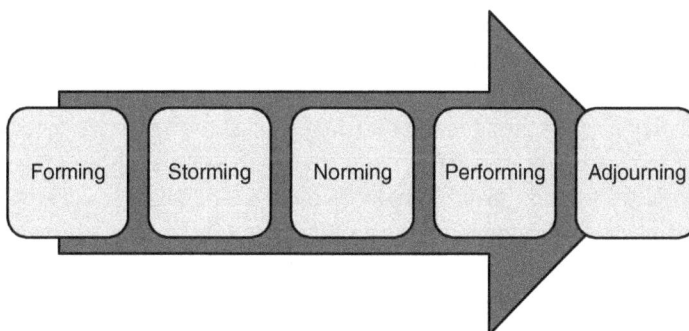

Figure 5.1   The FSNPA team building model

The stages of the model are summarised as:

> **Forming**: This is where a collection of individuals are called together and given a task to work on. Members start interacting and try to work out what is expected of them. Some members of the team will show excitement and enthusiasm, others will feel fear and uncertainty.

Storming: Conflict often occurs within the team as personal agendas come to light. As members assert themselves, they start questioning decisions and challenging authority.

Norming: During this stage, the group finds ways of resolving conflict and begin to emerge as a cohesive unit. Criticisms and feedback are given constructively and members start cooperating with one another.

Performing: Confidence grows both individually and with other members of the group as they work towards a common goal. They now begin to appreciate their role as a team.

Adjourning: Having completed their task, the team dissolves. This will be a great sense of loss or relief to the members depending on the outcome of the task.

Tuckman argues that, by understanding each of the stages and working through them in the sequence outlined above, the team will become a productive unit. Don't be fooled by the catchy terminology Tuckman uses to describe each of the stages, this really is a super model (even Tuckman's first and middle names, Bruce and Wayne, suggest as such). We are so impressed with this model that we've added two stages of our own: Scorning (where the individuals question the need for a team) and Yawning (where they become bored with the team's antics).

Here's another trip to the cinema to see the 1993 movie *Cool Runnings* to get an idea of what we mean by Tuckman's ideas:

Cool Runnings is a 1994 film loosely based on the true story of the Jamaican national bobsled team competing in the 1988 Winter Olympics. The team's coach, Irv Blitzer (wonderfully played by John Candy), won two gold medals for the bobsled for the USA in the 1968 Olympics. He pulls together an unlikely cast of characters, mostly made up of sprinters, to make up the team (*forming*). It's fair to say that none of the characters have any real aspirations to be Winter Olympians and there's a lot of animosity amongst members of the squad because of incidents that occurred when they were sprinting against each other (*storming*). They start to work cooperatively when they are looked down upon and ridiculed by other competing countries (*norming*). The early runs prove to be an embarrassment to the team as they finish last. Eventually, as they start to resolve the conflict within the team, they begin to operate as a cohesive unit and come close to breaking the world record (*performing*). They return home as great friends and heroes but never compete again as a team (*adjourning*).

It's in our additional stages (*scorning* and *yawning*) that your skills as a motivator will be put to the test (there's a number of entries in this book to help you out here).

You need to make it clear what the purpose of the group is, what their objectives are and the contribution they are making to the organisation. If boredom does become an issue, review the objectives and set new, challenging ones.

As the group begins to form they will become reliant on you for guidance, so give it to them! Negotiate and agree the ground rules, make the objectives perfectly clear, listen to any concerns they have and address these. Be prepared to deal with any baggage they bring to the group. It's important that you invest sufficient time in this stage as it will set the tone for the behaviours you want them to exhibit throughout the operational life of the team.

As they begin to deal with conflict, your role as motivator and director changes to one of supporter. This is where, as they begin to resolve issues, you need to provide support to those members who feel less secure. Avoid taking sides in the conflict and wherever possible allow them to resolve it. You may have to step in if it gets out of hand, but do this sparingly.

Once the group starts performing as a cohesive team don't be afraid to take a step back and let them get on with it. Once the task is complete, make sure you celebrate success and acknowledge everyone's contribution.

Susan Wheelan (2013) has built on Tuckman's FNSP model and suggested that teams achieve maturity simply through the process of working together. She claims that there is a significant relationship between the length of time that a group has been together and their behavioural patterns. She describes these relationships under four categories:

> **Dependency and inclusion**: Team members are dependent on the leader's direction and support. Conformity is high and members fear rejection.

> **Counter-dependency and fight**: Leadership authority is challenged. Conflicts about values emerge, disagreements occur and subgroups and coalitions are formed.

> **Trust and structure**: Roles and structures are formalised as the team starts to come together.

> **Work and productivity**: Performance improves as the team becomes clearer about their roles and objectives.

Wheelan has developed a group development observation system (GDOS) that assesses each member's perception of what stage the team's development is in. She suggests that changing your management style to match the developmental stage that the team is in is critical. We like the metaphor of parenting that Whelan uses to describe this model (see Figure 5.2).

In the first phase members display the characteristics shown in infancy: dependency, immaturity and a need to be wanted. Someone once reckoned that 80 per cent of what you need to learn in order to survive in life occurs in the first 20 per cent of your existence. Invest your time and efforts in this phase and be a good role model as to how you expect your team to behave.

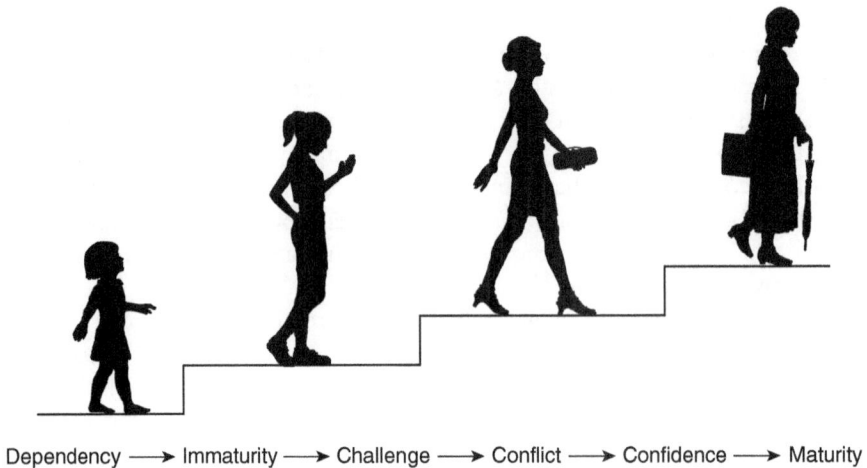

Dependency ⟶ Immaturity ⟶ Challenge ⟶ Conflict ⟶ Confidence ⟶ Maturity

Figure 5.2 The team maturity model

We now come to that wonderful phase known as adolescence (or parental purgatory in many cases). This is where you can expect conflicts about values, challenges to your authority, disagreements and fights. This is also where your patience, tolerance and understanding will be severely tested.

Getting through the adolescent phase unscathed is a major achievement but the job as team leader isn't complete. Backing off as your team enters the stage of young adulthood isn't going to be easy. In the interest of the team reaching maturity, however, learn not to get too involved as they begin to make decisions and take action.

CASE STUDY

New to her headteacher's post, Sarah quickly set about acquainting herself with the team that she had inherited, assessing their strengths and weaknesses to lead the changes that the school's performance indicated were necessary.

Sarah was forced to conclude that were she building a team from scratch, few of the present members would be obvious candidates and that even allowing for the talents of some, as a team they were definitely at the 'dependency' stage. Sarah therefore exercised great care in the selection of her first development project in order to promote less dependency upon her. Two other team members, Mike and Janet, who had demonstrated to her that they had real strength and expertise in the specific areas, were asked to take the lead on the project.

Everyone involved admitted that the outcomes were positive. The credibility of the project leaders was established at the same time as improving the confidence and expertise of other team members whose self-image received a much needed boost due to the successful accomplishment of the tightly defined roles they had been given.

Acting as a facilitator rather than a director is better here. Make sure that the team gets access to the resources they need to complete the task.

Maturity is where your team has the confidence and belief to tackle even the most challenging tasks that you present them with. Allow them space, don't interfere, but keep a watchful eye on them. Celebrate their achievements. They may have cut the apron strings but they will still look up to you and welcome your appreciation of their efforts.

As the result of a successful start, with careful nurturing and guidance from Sarah the team could move forward, growing in confidence towards becoming a more mature unit.

> **Hot Tip:** Accept that your role as team leader may change from control and direction to one of support and guidance as the project team grows in maturity.

The final word on teams:

- A group of individuals will need a common purpose and a sense of identity before they become a team.
- The characteristic of every team is influenced by the environment in which it functions. Look at the wider social, environmental and economic factors that will affect performance.
- Teams need to go through a stage of behaving in a manner expected by the team leader through a stage of doing things over and above what was expected in order to achieve increased productivity and personal development.
- Make sure that you have the right people in the right roles in your project team.
- Teams may need to go through the stages of *Forming*, *Storming*, *Norming*, *Performing* in order to achieve their successful completion of the set task.
- Teams can often achieve maturity simply through the process of working together.
- Accept that your role as team leader may change from control and direction to one of support and guidance as the project team grows in maturity.
- Be flexible in your team management style to suit the demands of the situation.
- Be adaptable in your management style to changes in circumstances.
- Learn how to adapt your management style to match the development stage of the group.
- Don't be afraid to revisit earlier stages in the team developmental process if you need to.

6

MOTIVATION

Dwight D. Eisenhower once said 'leadership is the art of getting someone else to do something you want done because he wants to do it'. While we're on the theme of great American generals, how about George S. Patton's belief that you 'Don't tell people how to do things, tell them what to do and let them surprise you with their results'. What enlightened leaders realise is that people are motivated by their own needs, expectations and interests but that they still have overarching tendencies and values that impact on their motivation to do things. Tapping into these values and knowing what they want and how they expect to be treated is what managers need to do to motivate their staff.

There are some really fascinating studies of motivation. We have chosen a theory that relates to motivation as a force that satisfies people's needs and two that examine how the way in which we treat people will motivate or demotivate them.

Arguably the most influential and often used theory relating to motivation is **Abraham Maslow**'s (1987) hierarchy of needs. Maslow's theory is usually presented in the form of a pyramid or series of steps that represents needs that must be satisfied in a sequential order from bottom to top (see Figure 6.1). He suggests that failing to satisfy a need at any level will prevent progression through to the next level.

The needs can be summarised as:

Physiological: These are basic to our individual and collective survival – food, water, warmth, rest.

Psychological: What we need to feel free from fear, to have certainty, stability and organisation.

Affiliation: To be a part of a relationship and to have a sense of belonging, affection and love.

Self-esteem: Self-belief generated through achievement, reputation and the respect of others.

Fulfillment: Reaching full potential.

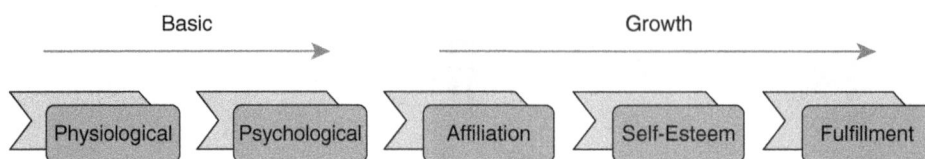

Figure 6.1   The hierarchy of needs model

The needs are divided into two categories: basic needs (physiological and psychological) and growth needs (affiliation, self-esteem and fulfillment). Maslow argues that we die if we fail to satisfy our basic needs, we feel inferior if our affiliation and esteem needs are unfulfilled, whereas self-fulfillment is our ultimate goal.

As a team leader you have a responsibility to ensure that your team's basic needs are met and to create a proper climate in which they can develop their full potential although establishing conditions to make this achievable may be challenging. Your responsibilities here are clear: make sure your team's basic needs are being met. These are broadly good working conditions and a safe working environment within the team, free from physical and psychological harm. Make sure that the school is an attractive place to work in and that heating, lighting and ventilation in classrooms meet the required standards. Compare working conditions with what goes on in other schools. If team members aren't dropping around you like flies or leaving in droves to join another school, then you can start working on satisfying some of their higher level needs. Start by encouraging social interaction and team spirit.

People are now feeling happy and content with life in your school. They are well-thought of members of a family with a good sense of security and belonging. Now comes the difficult bit. This is where you build up their self-esteem by designing challenging but meaningful tasks, giving positive feedback and praise, delegating responsibility and offering developmental training opportunities. Contentment now becomes excitement as people start to feel valued.

By now the model is nearly complete but putting the final touches to it may be beyond even the best of leaders. You can take people so far to reaching self-fulfillment by providing challenges and encouraging creativity but the motivation to get there may require a super-human effort. Both of us have known people who got within a whisker of reaching self-fulfillment only to self-destruct, and others that got there without realising it.

It is important that you realise that the final step depends on the individual's desire to want to get there and whether the environment in which they operate supports or hinders them. All you can do is make sure the foundations are solid enough to help them reach the peak. Without Sir John Hunt's meticulous planning and management, Edmund Hillary and Tenzing Norgay may not have had the physical or mental strength to have carved a place in history.

CASE STUDY

Few would have disagreed that Maggie was the very effective leader of a successful school. Her nurturing development of staff was recognised in her school's last two 'good' Ofsted judgements. Staff, parents and pupils liked and respected her and morale was high. Now was the time Maggie felt to move the school up to the next level. Unfortunately due to a mixture of over-expectation, misjudgment and bad luck this never happened. Rather the reverse occurred, threatening much of what had been accomplished.

In many respects Maggie was a victim of her past success. In taking staff to the level that she had, it had stretched some to their very limits. Consequently, higher expectations and increased demands proved too much for some. Two hard-working teachers simply did not have the skill-set to cope with additional demands. One integral middle manager could not balance increasing family commitments with increased responsibility, whilst Tom the assistant headteacher was going through a 'messy' separation from his partner.

Not long into 'the great push forward' cracks began to appear in morale and Maggie herself was aware that relationships with some staff were becoming more emotional and surprisingly on occasions even confrontational. Staff absence which used to be minimal began to become an issue and two long-term absences, one ending in a resignation, led to inconsistencies in teaching, resulting in dips in pupil achievement and behaviour and eventually a fall-off in parent satisfaction.

Maggie had the good sense to take stock and reflect on the evolving situation. She was able to draw upon the store of goodwill and respect that she had built over previous years to adjust course, trim demands and stabilise the school before the damage became permanent

Hot Tip: Don't think about your staff members' growth needs until you have satisfied their basic needs.

Motivating staff is simple to achieve but many leaders fail. This is because they think that it is their responsibility to constantly motivate staff when in fact all they have to do is create the environment in which staff can motivate themselves. **Frederick**

Herzberg et al. (2011) identified two groups of factors that cause either satisfaction or dissatisfaction. He called these motivators (job content) factors and hygiene (organisational context) factors.

> **Motivators** are generally concerned with the content of the job or nature of the work performed. In order to feel fulfilled, employees need to believe that their work has meaning. Motivational factors include: achievement, advancement, recognition and responsibility.

> **Hygiene factors** are usually associated with the context or environment in which the work is carried out. In order to feel content, but not necessarily fulfilled, the employee needs to be satisfied with general working conditions. Hygiene factors include: pay, company policy, status and security.

Herzberg refers to some of the erroneous beliefs that some organisations have about what motivates their employees as KITAs (kicks in the ass). These are defined as: negative physical KITAs (the literal kick up the backside); negative psychological KITAs (emotional games and manipulations) and positive KITAs (bonuses, pay increases, promotion). Herzberg argues that regardless of how good the KITAs were they will not on their own generate positive motivation. If they drop below an acceptable level, however, they will be the cause of demotivation.

If you want to give Herzberg's idea a chance, try the following:

- Make your staff's work interesting for them. Redistribute what may be considered the more mundane tasks between members of staff and impress on them the importance of their job to the organisation's overall performance.
- Give each member of staff the necessary resources and training to complete their job effectively. Make it clear that they are responsible for the quality of their work within their designated area of responsibility in the delivery and accomplishment of the school improvement plan, then give them the authority and autonomy to get on with it. Do this and they will see work as their responsibility and not something they have to do for the boss.
- Set challenging but realistic tasks which will give them a feeling of achievement and then recognise this publicly. Simply saying 'thank you' or 'well done' within earshot of as many staff as possible will do wonders for commitment and productivity.
- Provide opportunities for advancement and personal development for all staff. Promote from within the organisation whenever possible but remember that providing a new challenge or more interesting tasks can be just as strong a motivator as increasing pay or promotion.
- Although Hertzberg argues that factors such as pay and working conditions are not the main motivational factors, if they are unacceptable they can be serious demotivators. Compare working conditions and pay scales with other schools and ensure yours are comparable.
- Maintain good communications with staff and listen to what ideas they may have about their work.

CASE STUDY

As the time for Jim to transfer to his 'new' school came ever closer, he began to fret about whether he had done the right thing in leaving the safety of a 'comfortable' if rather modestly performing school. The move would give him the first taste of middle-leadership, but at what cost? His 'new' school had a history of poor performance, not to say 'difficult' pupils and parents. Would he be forsaking the enjoyment he had in his job?

As it turned out he need not have worried. Despite a tricky transitional first term of adjustment Jim could look back a year into the 'new' job with a considerable degree of satisfaction. It was a fact that some of his fears were realised; for example, the pupils did provide an additional degree of challenge to those he previously had to deal with. However, the additional commitment which it had been necessary to make was more than rewarded by the satisfaction that he felt from his new job. Like other staff, he was given a considerable degree of responsibility and though parameters and targets were always clear, the degree of autonomy allowed appealed to his creativity.

Jim had been challenged way beyond what had previously been asked of him but the buzz that he felt with the sense of achievement, not to mention the recognition from senior leaders, had added greatly to his sense of job satisfaction.

Hot Tip: Motivation is not always about pay and working conditions, very often it is about enrichment and fulfillment.

It is useful to have an understanding of the impact of Herzberg's KITAs. Equally important is the perception that you have of your team's motivation and what management style you adopt in dealing with this.

Douglas McGregor's (2006) Theory X and Theory Y sets out two theories by which managers perceive employee motivation. Each theory represents an extreme form of behaviour and can be summarised as the following:

Theory X suggests that most people:

- are driven by monetary concerns;
- will avoid work whenever possible;
- lack ambition and dislike responsibility;
- are self-centred and indifferent to organisational needs;
- have little aptitude for creativity and are resistant to change.

Theory Y suggests that most people:

- are driven by job satisfaction;
- actively seek work;

- show ambition and thrive on responsibility;
- are committed to achieving organisational objectives;
- have the capacity for creativity and welcome change.

McGregor proposed that all management practices stem from managers' perceptions of the basic nature of their team, thus creating Theory X and Theory Y managers. For example, a Theory X manager who believes employees will avoid work whenever possible will attempt to exercise control through close supervision, demands for strict adherence to rules and threats of punishment. A Theory Y manager, however, who believes employees actively seek work will create an environment where effort is recognised and rewarded.

Assuming that Theory Y managers are the ideal and that there is no place for Theory X managers is wrong. It sounds perfect being a Theory Y manager with Theory Y employees but let's be honest, this is the real world and we may have to deal with people whose motivation to work is purely to earn as much money as they can for as little effort as possible.

Under Theory X you can adopt either a hard or a soft approach to management. If you choose a hard approach then it will essentially be a command and control environment where you rely on coercion, implicit threats and tight supervision. If you choose a soft approach then cooperation, rewards and relaxed working conditions become the preferred working practices.

The optimal approach probably lies somewhere between 'command and control' and 'cooperation and collaboration'. Be flexible and adapt to changing circumstances if necessary, but be consistent in how you deal with people. Don't be the sort of manager who has one rule for one and another rule for another – this will get you into all sorts of trouble.

If Theory Y holds true then management becomes easier – wrong! If anything, managing becomes more challenging because you now have to deal with people with higher-level needs such as esteem and self-actualisation. In these circumstances use the employee's needs for fulfillment as the motivator by broadening the scope of their work, giving them added responsibility and involving them in decision-making. Foster creativity and ingenuity in Theory Y employees and delegate responsibility to them, but make sure they keep their feet on the ground as too much ambition and drive can be damaging to you and the organisation.

> **Hot Tip:** How you come over as a manager and react to your staff will have a massive impact on motivating them.

The final word on motivation:

- Leadership is the art of getting someone else to do something you want because they want to do it.
- Don't think about your staff members' growth needs until you have satisfied their basic needs.

- Motivation is not always about pay and working conditions, very often it is about enrichment and fulfillment.
- How you come over as a manager and react to your staff will have a massive impact on motivating them.
- Make your staff's work interesting for them.
- Give each member of staff the necessary resources and training to complete their job effectively.
- Make it clear that they are responsible for the quality of their work within their designated area of responsibility. then give them the authority and autonomy to get on with it.
- Set challenging but realistic tasks which will give them a feeling of achievement and then recognise this publicly.
- Simply saying 'thank you' or 'well done' within earshot of as many staff as possible will do wonders for commitment and productivity.
- Provide opportunities for advancement and personal development for all staff.
- Increased pay, promotion and improved working conditions on their own are not motivating factors.
- Although factors such as pay and working conditions are not the main motivational factors, if they are unacceptable they can be serious demotivators.
- Maintain good communications with staff and listen to what ideas they may have about their work.
- Progression to self-fulfillment depends on a stable foundation where lower-level needs are satisfied.
- Find out what makes people tick and develop strategies to get the best out of them.
- Motivating employees to achieve the best results for your organisation is about finding the right balance between command, control and cooperation.
- Motivation is all about matching effort to results, promising to reward people for the effort they make and never breaking your promises

7
STRATEGY

When Gilbert and Sullivan wrote the song 'I Am the Very Model of a Modern Major-General' for *The Pirates of Penzance*, they struggled to find a rhyme for 'strategy'. Having gone through various options, they settled for the line 'You'll say a better Major-General has never sat a gee' (mmm!). The problem that Gilbert and Sullivan experienced is nothing compared to those facing management in understanding the processes involved in planning successful strategies for their organisation.

We generally talk of strategy and tactics in terms of warfare; strategy being the processes of planning and directing military movements with the long-term aim of winning the war whereas tactics are specific techniques employed to win a battle or some section of a battle. In educational organisations, an operational strategy maps out the future for the organisation, setting out which services they will offer to which customers and decides how this will be done, by whom and when. In short, it sets the context for all management decisions.

Having an effective operational strategy will enable you to ensure the day-to-day decisions you make regarding your learners, your wider community, your staff, the educational authorities (local and national) and that they are in the best long-term interests of your organisation. In the entries that follow, we offer some interesting perspectives on the use of traditional analytical tools such as SWOT and PEST analysis. We then focus on a number of contributions to our understanding of relationships and dynamics in an educational context which will enable you to make strategic decisions regarding the most effective, efficient and economical positions for your organisation.

One of the problems with implementing operational strategies is that they are designed by organisational leaders and senior managers but implemented by middle and junior managers. Even with the best intentions and lines of communication, the former can become too obsessed with performance indicators and financial ratios and may lose sight of operational considerations. To be effective a good strategy encourages everyone in the organisation to work together to achieve a common aim. This was never more obvious than in the story of a group of US senators who were visiting NASA at the time when funding was under threat. One senator asked a man cleaning the floor, 'So what are you doing here?' The man answered, 'I'm here putting a man on the Moon!' That was his vision.

In medieval times, visions were frowned on to such a degree that having one would usually lead to an untimely end. Nowadays, not having a vision for your organisation is frowned upon, although the end may not be as painful as in medieval times.

Let's be clear here, if you are the leader of the organisation then this is your responsibility. If you have inherited a vision for where the previous leader thought the organisation should be going and it doesn't tally with the values that you or the community you serve hold, then you have to change it. Just a quick word of warning here: although you have the ultimate responsibility, don't impose a vision that you made up in the wee small hours of the morning – you will need to create a sense of organisational-wide ownership of the vision, so involve others in the creation of the vision.

A useful exercise here is to call an organisational-wide meeting. It could encompass staff, governors and representatives from parent organisations. Appoint a facilitator who has no prior connection with the organisation to oversee events and either join the group as a participant or sit back and watch proceedings. The facilitator should:

- Express the aims and objectives for the session and clarify what issues are non-negotiable, such as externally imposed achievement targets and procedures.
- Split the larger group into sub-groups of about five to seven people (ideally you want about seven groups, so do the maths). Have groups that are mixed representation and not all teachers in one group or all parents in another.
- Get each sub-group to draw an image (a metaphor) that describes the organisation as they see it now.
- Ask a representative from each group to describe the key features of their image.
- Draw a composite image from the contributions.
- Get each sub-group to draw an image that describes the organisation as they want it to be in three years' time.
- Ask a representative from each group to describe the key features of their image.
- Draw a composite image from the contributions.
- Phase one is now to focus on the second of the two images and to determine what the key components of the three-year image are. These will form the components of your vision.

From this activity a range of themes will emerge that will embody the values that underpin the organisation's vision. Articulate this vision in a short, simple and clear statement of intent (the mission).

Now you have a good understanding of where you want to be, it's time to take a step back and look at where you are. This is where you revisit the first of your two images. Here is one author's experience in acting out the facilitator's role:

CASE STUDY

The new principal of an adult and community college in the West Midlands completed the above exercise. Depressing images of ants crawling aimlessly over a dung heap, a broken-down school bus and a leaky watering can failing to get water to expectant plants were produced. The composite image was built around a half-empty school bus with miserable looking passengers, a driver who hadn't got a clue where she was going and a leaky radiator. The petrol gauge was showing nearly empty and the temperature gauge was well in the red. Had the radio in the bus been working, I'm sure the *Funeral March* would have been playing.

At this stage the facilitator decided we needed a break. He asked for the doors to be bolted to prevent the new principal from escaping. There was clearly a big job to be done to turn the college around.

(Cont.) The composite image for the college in three years' time was a properly serviced executive coach full of happy passengers. The petrol tank was full and Lewis Hamilton was driving it whilst being observed by the *Top Gear* team with their thumbs up smiling appreciatively (okay – we didn't draw this). Destination signs were clearly indicating which way to go. Although there were votes for Cliff Richard singing 'We're all going on a summer holiday' and Yazz singing 'The only way is up', the group thankfully settled on Queen singing 'Don't stop me now' as the accompanying music that was being downloaded.

From this we constructed the college's new mission statement:

(Cont.) The college's mission is to provide carefully planned teaching and learning that create a happy and caring environment which will stimulate learners to appreciate and achieve their full potential and make a valuable contribution to society.

Our next step was to begin to identify what courses of action were needed to get from the first image to the vision. Staying in the metaphorical world this involved having:

- A well-serviced coach.
- A driver who knows which are the quickest and best routes from A to B.
- Modern technology aboard the coach.
- A full petrol tank being replenished at every opportunity.
- Observers en route who are impressed by the bus and keen to get on board.

The trick is to now come back into the real world and to translate the images into real action. This is where we broke for a well-earned lunch.

After lunch we needed to take both an inward and outward look at the factors that would have an impact on moving the college from its present to its desired position. This is what **Gerry Johnson and Kevin Scholes** (2002) refer to as *posturing* and *positioning*. The next two sections will look at two tried-and tested-methods for doing this.

TAKING AN INWARD LOOKING PERSPECTIVE (*POSTURING*)

To demonstrate your understanding of the organisation's capabilities and the factors that exist within the micro-environment you need to conduct a SWOT analysis. The acronym stands for the **S**trengths, **W**eaknesses, **O**pportunities and **T**hreats that face an organisation seeking to change. It involves specifying the objective of the change and identifying the internal and external factors that are favourable and unfavourable to achieve that objective. Here are some possible factors that could indicate important influences for your project:

Strengths: Characteristics of the organisation that give it an advantage over others in fulfilling the national criteria for success.

Weaknesses: Characteristics that place the organisation at a disadvantage relative to others in failing to fulfill the national criteria for success.

Opportunities: *External* elements in the immediate environment such as potential partners (e.g. local businesses and specialist educational services) that could improve the prospects of success.

Threats: *External* elements in the immediate environment such as potential competitors (other schools, training providers and colleges) that could hinder the prospects of success.

Many SWOT exercises are undermined by a lack of rigour or clear perception of national expectations and contain overly optimistic statements about the organisation's current status and future prognosis. So how do you use SWOT analysis and avoid forming a plan that may be rejected as unrealistic?

Start by defining the focus of the plan. Ask yourself:

- What do I want my organisation to achieve?
- How does this compare with local or national expectations?
- Who are the customers of my organisation and what services do they want?
- What time scale do I propose for completion?

Once the focus is clear, select your SWOT team. Choose team members who can contribute to you being able to make an objective assessment of the internal factors that will affect the prospects of the plan being successful. Don't feel that you need to involve too many people in this stage, but do consider getting someone outside of the organisation to facilitate the session.

- Choose four or five people who have the necessary experience and knowledge of the organisation to contribute to the SWOT analysis.
- Think about drawing team members from different levels/departments in the organisation as this may give you a wider perspective of the situation.

Once the team is in place:

- Brief them as to the purpose of the meeting.
- Explain that the idea is to get a free and frank assessment of the factors that will affect future development. Make a special note that all contributions are welcome.
- Starting with the strengths, provide every member of the group with a supply of sticky notepads on which to record their ideas relating to the strengths of the organisation (you can brainstorm these ideas but we find self-stick notes work better).
- Ask them to stick these on the wall in a section designated 'Strengths'.
- Group the notes where there is some commonality in the suggestions.
- Follow this with weaknesses (or if you prefer, 'Areas for attention').
- Display these on the wall in a section designated 'Weaknesses'.
- Follow the same process for 'opportunities/threats'. Alternatively, you can go to the critical evaluation stage after the 'strengths/weaknesses' before moving on to 'opportunities/threats'.

Now move into the critical evaluation stage:

- Take each of the suggestions in turn and discuss its viability.
- Discard the ones that everyone agrees are not viable.
- Prioritise the ones that remain according to what their likely impact on the plan is going to be. Using a force field analysis (see the chapter on Managing Change) is a good way of doing this.
- Work down the list and decide what action you need to take to mitigate against weaknesses and threats and capitalise on strengths and opportunities.

Remember that one weakness or threat can wipe out all your strengths and opportunities or vice versa. IBM was in a powerful position to dominate the business computer industry in the 1980s. Because a weakness in their operation was that they didn't have the capacity to deliver the operating system they outsourced it to a young company called Microsoft. They made the mistake of selling them the licence for this for a measly US$50,000. In 2017, Microsoft was worth US$500 billion.

TAKING AN OUTWARD LOOKING PERSPECTIVE (*POSITIONING*)

To demonstrate your understanding of the macro-environment and the factors that may influence your ability to deliver a successful change programme, conduct a PEST analysis. This is concerned with the key external environmental influences on an organisation. The acronym stands for the **P**olitical, **E**conomic, **S**ocial and **T**echnological issues that could affect the implementation of the plan. Here are some possible factors that could indicate important external influences for your organisation.

> **Political**: Government expectations of education.
>
> **Economic**: Government spending, school annual budgets, funding opportunities.
>
> **Social**: Lifestyle changes (e.g. attitudes to education and leisure), health and welfare.
>
> **Technological**: New discoveries and developments, speed of technology transfer, impact of changes in information technology on the school.

Some analysts added **L**egal factors (including safeguarding and preventing extremism policies, environmental regulation and protection and employment law) and rearranged the acronym to SLEPT. Inserting **E**nvironmental factors (including ecological aspects such as the impact of climate change) expanded it to PESTLE. The model has also recently been further extended to STEEPLE and STEEPLED, by adding **E**thics and **D**emographic factors, but we think that we'll call it a day there.

Unfortunately most leaders or managers in smaller schools don't have the time to devote to complete a PEST analysis or may struggle to comprehend the importance of properly scanning the external environment. Simply compiling a list of external factors that might affect an organisation without critically analysing the full impact of these factors will contribute little to helping you to assess the feasibility of the project. The other side of the coin is that collecting a massive amount of information may lead to paralysis by analysis.

So how do you conduct an effective PEST analysis that will demonstrate an understanding of the context in which the project will operate?

Once the scope and scale of the study are clear, select a group of three to five people to form the PEST team. These can be drawn from middle- to senior-level staff within the organisation, or with limited availability of suitable personnel, and sufficient funds to do so, you may wish to commission the research from outside. Whatever you decide, choose people who have a good knowledge of the organisation and the sector in which it operates, and are capable of strategic analysis and thinking. Because the group will contain middle and senior managers or experienced consultants they won't lack the confidence to state their views, but you need to guard against one or two powerful personalities hijacking the meeting. If this is a problem consider appointing an outsider to act as facilitator, but brief them fully on their role and what you want out of the meeting.

Make sure that members of the team are not distracted by day-to-day matters. Hold the meeting off the school premises to avoid distractions. Use the process outlined in the SWOT analysis to generate a list of factors under each of the PEST headings that could impact on the project. Once the list has been generated, assess each idea against the following criteria.

- How likely is it to happen?
- What impact will it have on the project if it does happen?
- What strategies and/or resources do we need to minimise harm or maximise benefits should the event occur?

The combination of well-planned SWOT and PEST analyses is a really powerful activity that will contribute to either long-term strategic planning or short-term project development within the organisation (see the chapter on Project Management).

The final word on strategy:

- Ask what it is you want your organisation to achieve.
- Compare this with local or national expectations.
- Determine who the customers of your organisation are and what services they want.
- Decide the timescale for completion.
- Be clear about what the vision is for the organisation.
- Express the vision in a concise and compelling statement of intent.
- Celebrate small successes en route to achieving the vision.

8

MANAGING QUALITY

Ask a group of people to give you the name of a quality watch, car or school and the likelihood is that responses such as Rolex, Rolls Royce and Eton or Harrow will feature high on the list. This is because there is a tendency to measure quality in terms of price and prestige. The implications of this are that most people, unable to afford such luxuries, will be deprived of quality. It is important therefore that we measure quality not in the above terms but relative to *fitness for purpose*: will the product or service do what we want it to and is it accessible in terms of price and availability?

Educational leaders in the new millennium face a dramatic state of uncertainty. There is a great deal of pressure to achieve a range of performance expectations in a climate of student performance and financial accountability. Pressure is also mounting from those seeking to create alternatives to public education. How educational leaders perform the role of change agent may well determine the success and future of public schools. The direction for change must guide schools to be more productive, effective, efficient and human.

TOTAL QUALITY MANAGEMENT (TQM)

TQM was first introduced as a business management approach in the post-World War II era when an American statistician **William Edwards Deming** and others successfully reinvented the Japanese economy. Beginning in the early 1980s, business leaders looked to the philosophy and principles of TQM to find tools to improve the economy.

More recently, education leaders have begun to recognise the potential for TQM applied to educational organisations.

TQM provides a connection between outcomes and the process by which outcomes are achieved. If, as many people realise, the cause of failures in education is a problem in design, TQM may be regarded as an ideal systemic process for managing change in public education. There has been some reluctance to apply TQM practices that work in industry and commerce to education, yet central to Deming's methods and management philosophy is an insistence that anything can be made or done better.

For the purpose of this part of the book we want to concentrate on the aspects of TQM that relate to fitness for purpose and focus on the work of three theorists: William Edwards Deming, Phil Crosby and Vilfredo Pareto.

DEMING'S DEADLY DISEASES

The core of **Deming**'s (2000) work is what he referred to as the *Deadly Diseases* that had infected western organisations. These are:

A lack of constancy of purpose, which creates organisations that have no long-range strategy for staying in business. In education, Deming argued that we are plagued, at a macro level, by not having a clear purpose for schooling. His suggestion that the lack of a long-term definition ('What's the point of education?') and short-term thinking (how successive government ministers need immediate results) could not be more applicable than to schooling.

An emphasis on short-term profits, which undermines quality and productivity. Deming relates financial profit to student achievement and is very scathing in his accusation that schools are obsessed with standardised test metrics, which he fears is open to creative accounting.

Evaluating performance by using merit rating or annual review systems, which nurture inter-organisation rivalry and destroy teamwork. Deming argues that the merit system, and the suggestion to move towards payment by results for teachers, encourage short-term performance. He talks of the fear and bitterness that occur as the inevitable consequences of performance-related pay and annual appraisal, and how this is reflected in the increased demoralisation of teachers in countries which are introducing payment-by-results.

Mobility of management, which leads to a lack of understanding about the organisation and a reluctance to follow through on long-term objectives. According to government statistics the average lifespan of a teacher in the UK is about five years. In the UK we struggle to fill senior leadership posts. When a local primary school advertised their Head position in 1987, there were over 30 applicants. When the successful applicant retired in 2009, after 22 years in the post, there were only four applications.

Running the organisation on visible figures alone, which fails to recognise the importance of unknown and unknowable figures such as the 'multiplier' effect of a happy customer. Deming argues that this is perhaps the biggest indictment of the current education system. Replace the notion of a *happy/unhappy customer* with a *happy/unhappy learner*, and we're at the heart of the biggest distortion in our current school system. The present tendency is to judge a school only by a narrow, and wholly inappropriate, set of metrics. Deming suggests that if you ask a group of students how many of them would attend school if it wasn't compulsory, the average positive response would be about 30 per cent. He asks what business could survive if two-thirds of the customers were only there because they had to be. He claims that schools don't measure things like engagement or satisfaction with schooling partly because they don't want to know the results, partly because they don't know how to and partly because there's no reward for a good performance.

Deming argued that the above could only be tackled by effective leadership that demonstrated a commitment to quality, communicated the quality message to staff and recognised the need to create a belief in total quality management throughout its workforce. As Deming (2000) says, 'as long as education stays within politics, and so

CASE STUDY

Sara no longer teaches, although when she did she was recognised within her school, her local authority and Ofsted as an outstanding teacher and successful middle-manager.

A few years ago she was asked to lead the school's environmental agenda, a project that she took on with her usual commitment and with an added zeal reflecting her personal conviction in the importance of the issue. Her work was very successful and the school was beginning to be recognised for its environmental work.

An unfortunate blip in external test results meant that senior leadership hastily redeployed her talents in order to correct this. The excellent work that she had undertaken which had developed considerable environmental awareness among pupils was undermined by the person charged with replacing her, who was more concerned with prestigious, high-profile projects, that it must be said gained her personal recognition and did no harm to her career.

At least in part due to Sara's work test results did improve, but the preoccupation to preserve improvements often meant that she was continually working to a short-term agenda. This did little to contribute to her job satisfaction. Two years after her early retirement there was little trace of an environmental agenda at the school and results placed school achievement in the lowest 20 per cent of schools in the country.

long as the term of government is around 4–5 years, the push for short-term results is all we're going to get'.

I wonder what Deming would make of the UK phenomenon of the 'super head' who is lauded by government and brought in to provide a quick-fix to 'broken' schools before moving on to their next challenge?

> **Hot Tip:** Ask yourself: Is my organisation infected by one of the diseases? Do I see the cure as everyone's responsibility or restricted to senior management?

MOVE FROM UNCERTAINTY TO CERTAINTY

In expressing the notion that *Quality is Free*, **Phil Crosby** (1980) discussed the costs to organisations of providing goods or services that are not quality in terms of warranty claims and poor public relations. His belief was that an organisation that establishes a quality programme will see savings returns that more than compensate for the cost of the quality programme. Underpinning Crosby's belief was the principle of *'doing it right the first time'*, which he felt you only achieve once you reach a level of operational maturity which involves going through the stages shown in Figure 8.1.

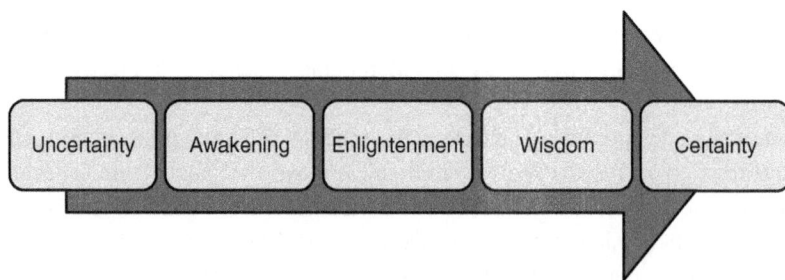

Figure 8.1   The uncertainty to certainty model

Each of these stages can be summarised as:

Uncertainty: Not knowing why you have a problem with performance quality, thus creating a tendency to want to blame others.

Awakening: Questioning if it's absolutely necessary to always have problems with quality, but not yet willing to devote resources to addressing problems.

Enlightenment: Through a management commitment to start identifying and devoting sufficient resources to start resolving problems

Wisdom: Believing in the value of defect prevention as a routine part of all operations.

Certainty: Knowing why you don't have a problem with quality.

Crosby argues that it is a 'long, long way from *uncertainty* to *certainty*. But travelling that road is what the fun of leadership is all about'.

Remember that the cost of quality is the expense of doing things wrong. Not knowing that you have a problem and inadvertently passing this on to your learners is a recipe for disaster. This will cost you dearly in terms of the loss of learner performance and a bad name in the community.

Start the journey from uncertainty to certainty by taking stock of where you are at this moment in time. Fill in the Quality Management Maturity Grid in Crosby's 1980 book, *Quality is Free* (there are numerous copies of this on-line). Don't just circulate this to senior members of staff to complete but to as many people as possible involved in the school (including governors, learners and their parents and the local community and business representatives). Ask them to be honest in their answers. If they have any concerns about reprisals get them to fill it in anonymously.

CASE STUDY

Helen's senior leadership team and governors left their feedback meeting following their inspection in shock. They were convinced that they were a good school and had found it hard to accept the verdict of the inspection team that they required improvement. Helen, who was relatively new to the school, was less certain that the inspection had got it wrong, but was sure that the 'required improvement' was not going to come about unless others became aware that despite what they may have thought, all was not well.

The inspection had in fact done her a favour in awakening others to the fact that despite what they might think other professionals had a very different view. The leadership culture needed to be changed from one of complacency to one of challenge. The initial key to this was overcoming insularity and raising awareness and expectation particularly in terms of how the school was judged in relation to key national performance indicators. When the reality of the school's situation was accepted, then the excuse menu could be replaced with a programme for identifying why the school was underperforming.

This was the school leadership's first foray into meaningful monitoring and discriminating evaluation and the results were rewarding, both in terms of school improvement planning and reshaping the perceptions and expectations of leaders. The subsequent heavy investment into monitoring and evaluation ensured that although perfection was not achieved, future visits and inspections brought no further surprises.

Don't be afraid if the general opinion is that you are in the early stages of maturity. Moving from unconscious incompetence (doing things wrong and being oblivious to it) to conscious incompetence (still doing things wrong but knowing you are doing it wrong) are the first steps you need to take. Accept that most things don't work like they are supposed to work, but remember that problems with any aspect of the school breed problems and the lack of a disciplined approach to openly attacking them breeds more problems.

Attacking the cause of the problem needs to be precise and accurate and you need to measure the right things in terms of staff and learner needs. Remember it only takes one bad bit of data to compromise the integrity of the whole exercise. Don't get lost in statistical swamps but do get a complete picture of the problem and then make sure you devote adequate resources to addressing it.

Of course, the proof of excellence is in the *prevention* of problems, not fixing them. Define your staff and learner requirements and agree performance standards before you start delivering and then make absolutely sure nothing will happen to compromise delivery. If you have a limited amount of time to be able to devote to dealing with these problems, then use a process such as the Pareto Principle (see below) to manage your time more effectively.

> **Hot Tip:** Believe in the value of defect prevention as a routine part of all operations within the organisation.

DEAL WITH THE VITAL FEW, NOT THE TRIVIAL MANY

The *Pareto Principle* was devised in the late-19th century by the Italian economist Vilfredo Pareto. He first used it to demonstrate that 80 per cent of the wealth in Italy was owned by 20 per cent of the population. It was **Joseph Juran** (1967), one of the TQM quality gurus who, some seventy years later, stumbled across his work and helped to popularise its use. It is possibly the single most useful theory that a manager can know about. Why? Because it can be used to significantly reduce a manager's workload and is applicable in a huge range of circumstances.

This theory of 'the vital few and the trivial many' does not pretend to be a precise measure of any phenomena. The split may be 70/30 or 90/10. It's a rule of thumb which can be applied to a wide range of questions relating to staff, products, resources, customers and suppliers, but the precise split will differ from instance to instance.

Here are just two examples of how you might use the Pareto Principle:

- 20 per cent of your staff cause 80 per cent of your problems. Sort them out and leave the others to get on with it.
- 20 per cent of your staff contribute 80 per cent of your success. Make sure you reward them!

The one commodity that managers lack more than any other is time. Any theory that will save you time and help direct your efforts to where they will have the greatest impact has to be a winner. This is what the Pareto Principle does; it separates the important few from the unimportant many. It shines a light on those few processes and people that cause you most of your problems. Sort out the 20 per cent causing problems and watch your 'to do' list shrink.

The Pareto Principle is extremely elegant in its simplicity and has shown over the years that it can be applied to virtually any situation. Of course the split may not be exactly 80/20, but it will be in that ball park. Try it out on a range of issues and prove for yourself how all-pervasive the ratio appears to be.

CASE STUDY

Gill and her senior management team, with help from an external consultant, agreed that teaching and learning in the school required improvement. Gill imagined a visit (heaven forbid) the following week from Ofsted which would come to the same conclusion and of her delivering the verdict to staff when the report was published. She pictured that moment in the staffroom and the reactions of individual members of staff. Was this overall judgement on the quality of teaching and learning fair on the majority of them? Patently no, for there was much good teaching within the school. It was the teaching of a minority of the staff that was holding the school back.

Gill was determined to avoid one-fix-fits-all measures, for example adopting new methodologies or new schemes across the board, and to concentrate instead on the performance of identified individuals. Taking this individual approach further, she adopted different approaches to suit the individuals concerned. Gill could not claim 100 per cent success, after all that would have achieved an outstanding grade for teaching and learning at the school's inspection a year later. However, the judgement of 'good' was ample reward for the approach she elected to use.

Hot Tip: Concentrate your energies on dealing with the vital few rather than the trivial many.

The study of quality can be a complicated matter. It has, according to Phil Crosby, much in common with sex: everyone is for it (under certain conditions of course); everyone feels they understand it (even though they wouldn't want to explain it); everyone thinks its execution is only a matter of following natural inclinations (wouldn't it be wonderful if it was?); and, of course, most people feel that all problems in these areas are caused by other people. It is difficult to have a meaningful discussion on sex, quality or other complex subjects until some basic assumptions are examined. This is what this chapter is all about. By reading it you will have not only a much better understanding of what quality is all about and how to manage it, but also some useful tools that you can apply. I don't know what help it will be to your sex life, however.

> **Hot Tip:** Measure quality in terms of fitness for purpose: does it do what it says it will do on the tin?

The final word on managing quality:

- Measure quality in terms of fitness for purpose, not luxury or prestige.
- Understand where the root cause of your quality problems is.
- Quick-fix solutions on quality issues aren't always the best.
- Concentrate your energies on dealing with the vital few rather than the trivial many.
- Believe in the value of defect prevention as a routine part of all operations within the organisation.
- Make sure that quality management is everyone's responsibility, not restricted to senior management.

9

HUMAN RESOURCE MANAGEMENT

Forget about having the latest technology or a new lick of paint throughout the building, your people are your greatest asset and should be dealt with accordingly. When we started to put together this section, we chose personal qualities that we felt we would look for in a leader. These are: someone we can trust, who will challenge us with good intent, who encourages us to be creative, who recognises and rewards our talent and who can remain calm when under pressure or dealing with conflict. Let's look at some interesting theory that underpins these qualities.

TRUST

Stephen Covey (2004) uses the analogy of making deposits and withdrawals in a bank account to demonstrate the interactions that we have with other people that result in trust – deposits being when we do something good for the other person and withdrawals when we do something bad. He states, however, that unlike a bank where we may only have one or two accounts, we have an *emotional bank account* (EBA) with each person that we come into contact with. He highlights five major deposits that build up the EBA:

- Understanding the individual.
- Attending to the little things.

- Keeping commitments.
- Clarifying expectations.
- Showing personal integrity.

Failing to act in accordance with any of the above may constitute a withdrawal. It is inevitable, however, that there will be occasions when you have to make a withdrawal. If this happens, then Covey suggested a sixth deposit may be possible if you explain why you did what you did and, if necessary, apologise sincerely.

CASE STUDY

Karen prided herself on taking the time and trouble to 'know' her staff and for many years had made time before and after school to chat with them individually. This was invaluable in understanding them and helping inform her expectations of them. It meant that she was responsive and sympathetic and helped her to get the best out of them. However, the demands of a difficult year, including long-term staff absences and her involvement in helping another local school that was having problems, had severely restricted her time for socialising and she had failed to ensure that other leaders were maintaining informal communication networks.

Her decision to move one of her best teachers, Rita, from her Y2 duties to teach in Y6 was therefore not informed by her background knowledge. Half-term Y6 data, lesson observations and book scrutinies indicated that Rita's move was not the success that Karen had thought it would be. Initially this was put down to Rita's unfamiliarity with the new situation, but as the term wore on further worrying signs became apparent, most alarmingly Rita's deteriorating relationships with some pupils and her general negativity which had never before been the case. Early into the second term things came to a head, when Rita began what turned out to be quite a lengthy absence due to anxiety. In part this was the consequence of a crisis in confidence brought about by being propelled into a new situation for which she herself was not adequately prepared due to events in her private life.

As the circumstances gradually came to light, Karen was left to reflect on the effect that her decision had on Rita, the pupils in her class and the knock-on effects on the school. Before her return to work, discussions with Rita revealed that she felt that she had been let down and treated unsympathetically. Karen was forced to agree that she had, by her own high standards, been negligent in failing to understand Rita's situation, and in focusing on the 'big picture' had taken her eye off those important, if more minor, factors and told her so. Fortunately the effects were short term; because of her 'track-record' Karen's stock was high and Rita and others could accept that as ever her motives were sincere.

Sadly, even with your support, your staff will sometimes fail to achieve set tasks or have to be warned about aspects of their behaviour. If your *emotional bank account* is sufficiently high with them, and you explain why the action was necessary, you can even turn a withdrawal into a deposit. Don't try doing this with the bank though.

> **Hot Tip:** Always listen to what your staff have to say. Make sure that what you have to say is understood, not just heard. Act with integrity and never try to play one member of staff off against another.

CHALLENGING

Learning to challenge someone with the intention of developing them rather than putting them down is one of the key attributes that define professional behaviour. The concept of neuro-linguistic programming (NLP) was developed in the early 1970s by **Richard Bandler** and **John Grinder** (1979) with this intent in mind.

The breakdown of the term defines what NLP is all about:

Neuro is how you use your senses to make sense of what's happening, which in turn influences how you feel and the level of challenge you can exert on someone.

Linguistic is the language and communication systems that you use to challenge and influence yourself and others.

Programming is a succession of challenging steps designed to achieve a particular outcome.

Bandler and Grinder stress that anyone involved in any relationship can use NLP techniques to have a positive influence on the person that they are challenging. Here are some important principles should you chose to use NLP as a management tool:

The map is not the territory: Accept that, if the territory represents reality, the map is merely the representation of that reality by the person you are challenging.

Respect the other person's map: Acknowledge that everyone responds according to their individual maps and may act in ways that you find unhelpful or unacceptable.

The meaning and outcome of the challenge is the response that you get: Instead of blaming staff for misunderstanding your meaning and not responding to your challenge, accept total responsibility for your communication.

Every behaviour has a positive intention: Appreciate that behaviour is created specifically with regard to the context and the reality currently being experienced. Change is necessary when the context and the reality change.

Accept the person, change the behaviour: Understand that the behaviour of staff is not who they are. Accept the person but support them to change their behaviour.

There is no failure, only feedback: Reassure staff that if they haven't succeeded in something, they haven't failed, they just haven't succeeded yet. Challenge them to vary their behaviour and find different ways of achieving their desired outcomes.

If you always do what you've always done, you'll always get what you've always got: This is sometimes referred to as **Ashby**'s (1956) *Law of Requisite Variety*. Recognise that the individual with the greatest flexibility of thought and behaviour is more likely to control the outcome of any interaction.

CASE STUDY

Jill was not looking forward to the departmental meeting. She knew that Lynne was not going to take kindly to the wholescale changes she proposed to teaching within her department. Lynne was set in her ways and could be relied on to be resistant to change, however slight and well-intentioned. The fact that results were below par would not deter her from blaming others, rather than embracing the fact that change was needed. The meeting could be explosive and Jill felt that whatever the outcome, Lynne would be a barrier to change, for there were others who, though less vocal, would be sympathetic to her views.

Jill decided to have a one-to-one discussion with Lynne prior to the meeting at which she would try to establish common ground by exploring the issues and persuading her of the imperative to raise pupil achievement. Somewhat to her surprise there was little debate about this. Lynne's objection was to the means of improvement - after all, she claimed, what was wrong with current practice? She was achieving good results with the pupils she taught. If only others within the department could do the same (she didn't hesitate to identify those very teachers).

Reflecting on the meeting Jill was forced to agree that Lynne had a point. After all, despite her methods being somewhat 'old-school' she invariably achieved the best results. Jill thought that maybe she ought to monitor teaching and learning within the department further to try to explain some of the anomalies that existed between her perceptions of staff and their actual outputs. Her evaluations convinced her that in going ahead with her radical changes, she would be pandering to the 'bright-young things' within her department at the risk of alienating those who were actually delivering results.

The radical changes were never proposed at the meeting and subsequent improvements in achievement were the result of targeting individual teacher performance.

Hot Tip: Ask yourself: How is my sense of reality different to the person I am managing? Am I sure that the person I am managing fully understands what I want them to do? Do I make sure they learn from any failures they experience?

ENCOURAGING CREATIVITY

Edward De Bono (2009) argues that in order for leaders to be more creative in the way that they approach problems, they have to get a more rounded view of a situation and have to move outside of their habitual thinking modes. He developed his *Thinking Hats* technique as a means of encouraging people to be more rounded and creative in the way they approached solving problems. In this technique you simply wear the hat (actually or figuratively) depending on which approach you need to adopt. These are categorised as:

White Hat: Focus on the information available; get them to see what they can learn from this.

Red Hat: Rely on intuition and emotion; get them to try to understand the responses they get.

Black Hat: Look at the negative points; get them to try to see the weaknesses in an idea.

Yellow Hat: Look at the positive points; get them to try to see the strengths in an idea.

Green Hat: Develop creative solutions; encourage them not to be afraid to make suggestions no matter how off-the-wall they seem.

Blue Hat: Take control of the situation; show them how this helps them to get things going when they start to stall.

De Bono argues that most people approach dealing with problems from a rational, positive viewpoint. Often, though, they may resist using their emotional, intuitive or creative capacities, which can result in barriers to learning or a failure to make creative leaps. He suggests that the Thinking Hats technique is a good way of getting people to think outside the box and encourages them to be creative in how they deal with problems. Let's see how you can use this to address a problem in education in a developing world village:

CASE STUDY

The Wonder Years Centre of Excellence (WYCE) supports the development of health-care and education in Medina Salaam, a small village in The Gambia. Over the past thirteen years, WYCE has built a primary school that has over 300 pupils, a health centre, wells, gardens and even a football pitch. The charity provides the salaries for the 12-strong teaching staff in the village. Working in collaboration with the Gambian Teaching Union, WYCE is looking to develop a teacher-training programme that will enhance the abilities of the teachers in the village.

Here's how you can use the Thinking Hats technique to work with a group of teachers in the UK to help develop this programme:

- Wear the *blue hat* as you explain to the group what's required from the session.
- Get your group to start with *white hat* thinking by looking at the data that you have collected from analyses of the situation. This will include other trends in learning used in the village, what technologies they have and what cultural issues there may be.
- Get the group to change to *red hat* thinking and shout out ideas for delivering teacher training in the village. Make sure that you list every suggestion.
- Look at each suggestion in turn and ask the group to put on *black* or *yellow hats*, depending on whether they disagree or agree with the idea. Score each suggestion depending on the numbers of *red* and *yellow hats* that you see.
- Once you have a consensus of *yellow hat* wearers on any idea then turn to *green hat* thinking for creative thoughts on how to turn the idea into a reality.
- Don't be afraid to hand the *blue hat* to another member of the group if you feel your leadership isn't working or you need a different perspective.

This was a real-life situation that one of us was involved in and which we have used to demonstrate how the Thinking Hats approach works. Now look at how you can apply the technique on things such as curriculum design or team building. If you want to use the Thinking Hats process, you may find that making hats may be time consuming or expensive. We use a set of table tennis bats (brought in packs of three) from one of those high street pound shops. Strip off the rubber and paint them in the six colours. People just pick up the bat that reflects their thoughts. Coloured cards work just as well but don't have the same aesthetic appeal.

> **Hot Tip:** Ask yourself: Have I got the group to think creatively? Have I listened attentively to their responses? Have I made sure that I have sought feedback and am prepared to act on this?

APPRECIATING TALENT

Lawrence Peter and **Raymond Hull** (2009) proposed the *Peter Principle*, which suggests that people are promoted to their highest level of competence, after which further promotion raises them to a level just beyond this and they become incompetent (see Figure 9.1).

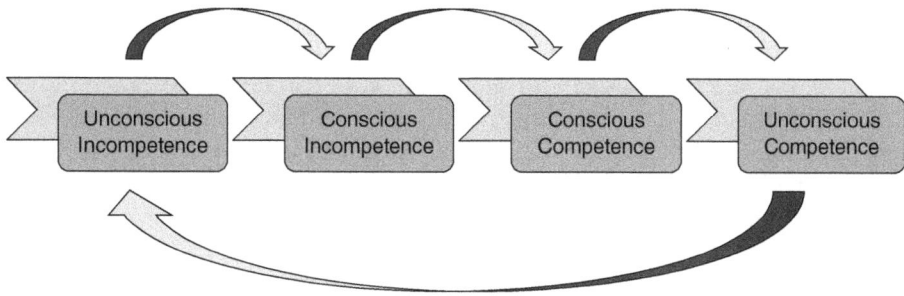

Figure 9.1 The competence model

The Peter Principle levels are:

Unconscious incompetence: Someone who doesn't know how to do something, but is totally oblivious to the fact that they don't know this. To reach the next level, they need to know what it is that they don't know.

Conscious incompetence: They now know what it is they want to do, and start to appreciate the gap in their competence. To reach the next level they need to know how to become competent.

Conscious competence: Now they can do what it is they need to do, but have to give it a lot of attention. Through repeated practice they can reach the next level.

Unconscious competence: At last they can perform a skill easily without giving it a great deal of thought. Once unconscious competence is achieved, they are at a level which suits their ability at that moment in time.

Unconscious incompetence: The danger now is that complacency in their present role might result in a return to the first level.

The usefulness of this theory is in challenging the belief that the selection of a candidate for promotion should be based on their performance in their current role, rather than on their ability relevant to the intended role. Here are six ways to beat the Peter Principle:

- Don't fall into the trap of believing that competence in someone's current role suggests they will be competent in a higher-level role. Good teachers don't necessarily make good curriculum leaders.
- Match the person's capabilities with the demands of the job. Your starting point should be an analysis of the skills required to achieve success in the new role. Good admin officers don't necessarily make good teaching assistants.
- Talk to staff about their career expectations and interests about holding a higher position. This will help in analysing where they would like to see themselves and whether they are satisfied with their current role or not. In this way they won't be compelled to do something that they are not comfortable about.

- Accept that it's not always necessary to promote a member of staff who is good in their existing job. Sometimes, without any significant change in their responsibilities, you can reward them for their hard work by offering other incentives.
- Don't be afraid of demoting or sacking people who have reached their level of incompetence. This may sound harsh but it can be a win–win situation because the individual who is at their level of incompetence may welcome an opportunity to return to what they did well (provided there was a face-saving way to do it).
- If you have promoted an individual and discover that they are not competent at that level, by organising for them to have additional training, mentoring or shadowing someone who is competent you give them the tools they need to succeed.

This theory has been interpreted by different people over time. **Scott Adams** (1996), a brilliant satirist and cartoonist, proposed *The Dilbert Principle* based around the concept that in many cases the least competent, least smart people are promoted to management level simply because they're the ones you don't want doing the actual work. He claimed that you want managers doing the easy work like 'ordering the doughnuts and yelling at people for not doing their assignments' and that 'your smart people, the heart surgeons and the computer programmers aren't in management'. Of course we're not suggesting for one minute that this applies to you, but we both like jam doughnuts.

> **Hot Tip:** Don't be afraid to recognise that you have faults that need to be addressed. Ask others to give you feedback on your performance. Never get complacent. Thinking there's no room for improvement is a recipe for disaster.

DEALING WITH CONFLICT

We have news for you! Conflict within organisations is inevitable. You can deal with this in a *fight or flight* manner. If you fight, be wary of the victims (you may be one of them). If you flee, then be aware that you may only be putting things off. If things do escalate because you didn't deal with them immediately, a minor skirmish may turn into full-scale war.

To help you resolve conflict we want to look at two models which will help you to (a) understand how conflict arises and (b) have a strategy for dealing with it.

Steven Karpman (1968) devised the Drama Triangle model to plot the interplay between two or more people. The model is based on Eric Berne's (1964) Transactional Analysis theory that people act out a 'script' which is composed of their understanding of who they are and what the world is like. Three characters make up the script:

Victim: A character who usually feels overwhelmed by their own sense of inadequacy and impotency. They look on themselves as being powerless to resist those wanting to take advantage of them.

Persecutor: Someone who has the power to take advantage of the victim but is often unaware that they have this power. Racked by doubt, they often feel they are the ones being persecuted.

Rescuer: Rather than recognising their own failings, this is someone whose mission is to rescue others. They look on themselves as being used and unappreciated.

Karpman sets the scene for the 'drama' as a series of complementary transactions that continue amicably providing it suits both parties. The drama reaches a climax when one actor becomes disoriented and switches roles. Whilst it was originally intended as a therapeutic tool, the Drama Triangle can also be applied in management.

In order to know how to use it effectively, you need to know how you first got hooked into the drama. Think of a situation that got really messy for you or your staff. How did it start? Was it a simple question, a comment or a criticism? Whatever hooked you, which of Karpman's roles did you assume? If you felt the need to protect someone, you were probably the rescuer. If you were upset by their comments, you clearly looked on yourself as the victim. If you were to blame for the other person's problems, then you may have felt that you were the persecutor.

Let the drama commence. You now begin to immerse yourself into the role. The other characters do the same. The drama either follows a well-staged production with the victim becoming suicidal, the persecutor assuming Karloffesque (maybe Kruegeresque is more contemporary) proportions and the rescuer becoming a super-hero. Job done, BAFTA nominations all round. What happens, however, if someone varies from the script and the persecutor racked with guilt becomes the persecuted or the superhero feeling unappreciated becomes the villain or the victim fights back and becomes a persecutor? Now it gets interesting.

Sorry, we forgot you are a manager not a film director. Using this analogy, however, can be a very powerful way of understanding how interactions take place. Not all victims remain victims and not all persecutors stay as persecutors. You also need to be aware that not all people looked on as victims perceive themselves in that way. The same can be said for persecutors and rescuers. Your role is to dig deep into what's motivating the individual to act in the way that they are acting.

Don't think that it's your responsibility to change the way they are thinking or acting. Let them have the responsibility for this. They may draw comfort in the role they have assumed; they may not even be aware of how people are viewing their role. Whatever the circumstances changing roles, if necessary, is down to them. Support them to do this only if necessary.

Kenneth Thomas and **Ralph Kilmann** (1974) suggested five approaches that can be used to resolve conflict within the workplace. In their model they categorised each approach in accordance with levels of *assertiveness* and *cooperation*. They described the consequences of each approach as:

Avoiding: Neither party being satisfied.

Accommodating: One party sacrificing their own needs to satisfy the needs of the other party.

Compromising: Both parties being partially satisfied.

Competing: One party winning at the expense of the other.

Collaborating: Both parties being fully satisfied.

Thomas and Kilmann argued that understanding the possible consequences of each approach will enable you to select which one to use.

> **Hot Tip:** Accept that neither you, nor your staff, are perfect and have flaws. Never allow your personal feelings for a member of staff to affect the way you deal with them.

CASE STUDY

Looking back on his first term as headteacher Gurdip could, with typical modesty, reflect with a good deal of satisfaction on what had been achieved. Most importantly, as far as he was concerned, the staff after initial suspicion and reluctance to embrace change appeared to be on-side. Gurdip thought it would be a good time to give middle leaders a higher profile and concluded that a simple and undemanding way to do so would be to timetable each leader to front one school assembly each half-term.

Gurdip did not anticipate the response, typified by Vikram who had been one of his first 'converts'. Despite his many qualities he simply could not cope with the idea of standing up in front of the whole school. Concerned about perceptions if he backed down from one of his first, and to his mind least threatening initiatives, Gurdip tried to reassure him, but to no avail; the idea simply terrified him. He could not be 'reasoned' with and as pressure from Gurdip mounted the situation turned from emotional to confrontational, with Vikram threatening union intervention to prevent what he saw as bullying.

Popular among staff, Vikram's objections were viewed sympathetically by them to the extent that Gurdip felt cornered and the victim in the situation. He had genuinely been attempting to develop the role of his middle leaders in a sympathetic manner but feared he was now seen as persecuting Vikram.

CASE STUDY

Bob had led programmes involving learners of all ages in schools, colleges, universities, training organisations, even prisons and bail hostels. It was very rare that he had encountered conflict in any of the programmes he had been involved in that had resulted in violence between members of his teams, but on one occasion (involving two elderly members of his team) that it did happen, Bob decided that he had to act decisively and exclude the perpetrator from his team. It was the only fair thing to do! Or was it?

Bob realised some twenty years after the event that he had acted instinctively. His default position was that violence was unacceptable, a risk to the health and safety of others and that exclusion from the team was the only solution.

Bob freely admits that he didn't like the perpetrator: she was a bit odd and not popular with other members of the team. Excluding her went down well with the rest of the group and there was some sense of self-satisfaction, as Bob had a tendency to try to avoid confrontation.

Now what do you think – was he being fair?

To be fair, you need to:

- Identify what your default position is; fight or flight.
- Gather as much information as you can about the circumstances that have led to the conflict.
- Approach the situation in a calm and assertive manner.
- Listen to what all concerned in the conflict (observers as well as contributors) have to say.
- Make an assessment as to which approach you need to adopt.
- Set out the facts and explain why you have adopted the approach you have.
- Try to remain non-confrontational and focus on the issue not the person.

No need to send us a postcard with your answer to whether or not Bob was being fair. We're not sure that the end result would have been any different but, had one of your erstwhile authors acted in line with the above, he may not have been questioning himself some twenty years later.

The ability to manage your emotions and remain calm under pressure has a direct link to your performance. An important aspect of exuding calmness is your ability to

Hot Tip: If conflict does arise, act in a calm manner and gather as much information as you can about the incident. Focus on the issue, not the person.

control stress. Notice we use the phrase 'control stress' not eradicate it: you need stress to function effectively. Yoga and Tai chi are techniques to use to control stress that have been in existence for over 2,000 years. *Mindfulness* is one of the newer ideas relating to stress control.

Mindfulness means knowing directly what is going on inside and outside yourself, moment by moment. Although mindfulness is based on some of the principles of Buddhism, it was the work of **Jon Kabat-Zinn** (1994) in the mid-1990s that popularised it as a tool for controlling stress. According to Kabat-Zinn, mindfulness is about dealing with thoughts in a detached, de-centred and non-judgmental manner. The main characteristics when managing in stressful situations are:

Be non-judgmental: Don't allow your own goals and values to affect your judgement on what's happening. The temptation is to judge each action by the individual as good or bad. By letting go of these judgements, you will see things as they are, rather than filtering them through your own personal belief system.

Focus on purpose: Learn to manage the discomfort of uncertainty. Don't get sidetracked and become stressed when things don't go right. Stay focused on the task in hand. Accept that there will be dark moments when you feel there is little hope. If you allow this negativity to take over completely, however, your staff will pick up on this and all of you will get into a downward spiral.

Live in the present moment: Learn to slow down, ignore negative brain chatter about the situation troubling you and experience the event for what it is. Being in the 'here and now' means that you experience things for what they are and not what they have been or might be.

CASE STUDY

Jack exercised great care in identifying, cultivating and training members of his senior leadership team. Amongst the characteristics he most prized were individuality and strength of character to voice their opinions, even when they were not in agreement with his own. He valued alternative viewpoints which provided him with balance, cautioning, providing alternatives and also positivity when most needed.

There was an occasion when Jack was exercised about a member of staff who he thought was being obstructive. Steve was not only able to offer an alternate viewpoint regarding the motives of this member of staff, but was also capable of dealing with them in a more sensitive manner and one which achieved a successful outcome. The investment in time spent by Jack in surrounding himself with dependable people such as Steve was rewarded by the avoidance of stress and negativity in situations such as this.

Central to Kabat-Zinn's theory is the notion of using meditative techniques to stay in the body and to observe what thoughts are going on in the mind but not to identify with them. Someone once told us that if you can't find twenty minutes to meditate each day, find an hour.

Most people accept that taking time over their hygiene (showering, brushing teeth) or exercising is essential but ignore the care and attention needed for their greatest asset; their mind. The mind can be the source of happiness or despair, creativity or self-destruction or problem-solving or problem-making.

> **Hot Tip**: Learn how to control, not eradicate stress.

The final word on managing human resources:

- If you lack confidence in your management ability, talk to people who can help you to improve this.
- Never get complacent: thinking there's no room for improvement is a recipe for disaster.
- Never allow your personal feelings for a member of staff to affect the way you deal with them.
- Learn how to control, not eradicate stress.
- Acting creatively is about thinking outside of the box.
- Don't be afraid to recognise that you have faults that need to be addressed.
- Ask others to give you feedback on your performance.
- Ask yourself: Am I sure that the person I am managing fully understands what I want them to do?
- Do I make sure they learn from any failures they experience?
- Ask yourself: Am I sure that I am in the right frame of mind when I communicate with the person I am managing? Do I appreciate what frame of mind they are in?
- Accept that neither you, nor your staff, are perfect and have flaws.
- Always listen to what your staff have to say. Make sure that what you have to say is understood, not just heard.
- Act with integrity and never try to play one member of staff off against another.

10

MANAGING BUDGETS

The ability to create an accurate budget for a school, whether it involves the budget for a small-scale project like an after-school club or something major like the yearly overall budget, and then to manage it is an essential skill for a budget holder. In our experience this can be a daunting task, especially if the budget holder is new to the role.

It's important here to draw the distinction between one-off projects, where there is scope for negotiations on the budget, and the overall operating budget, which may be a sum pre-determined by the authorities. Although the process described below relates more to one-off projects (which may or may not be the Head's direct responsibility), it can also be applied equally to the overall school budget (which will certainly be the Head's direct responsibility) and secondary budgeting where departmental or curriculum leaders bid for their share of the overall budget.

ESTIMATING HOW MUCH YOU NEED

As a budget holder one of the first questions you may be asked by senior management or the school governors (or external funding bodies such as Sport England or the Lottery) is 'How much is it likely to cost?'. One of the first questions you may want to ask them is 'How much are you going to give me?'. Wouldn't it be great if the answers to both questions were the same? Unfortunately life isn't quite like that. You need a ballpark figure to kick off the negotiations with. Here are some thoughts to help you with this.

Here is an example of estimating project costs that were way off target:

The Australian company that rebuilt Wembley football stadium quoted £458m for the project. It cost £827m. You may think that the company did well out of the deal. Well, not quite - they made a loss of nearly £150m. This means the real costs of the project were well over double the estimates.

Okay, you're probably not looking at a project worth anywhere near a billion pounds but, even if it runs into hundreds, you will want the gap between projected and actual costs to be as small as possible. You will also want to make sure that you have sufficient funds to deliver the goods. The thought of having to keep playing the FA Cup Final in Cardiff (as wonderful as the Millennium Stadium and Welsh hospitality are) was too horrendous to contemplate had the government pulled the plug on the Wembley project because of the disparity between actual and projected costs.

One way of achieving this when dealing with one-off projects is to over-estimate the costs and pay back any excess at the end of the project. This carries two risks: the first is that potential funding bodies may reject the project on the basis that it is too expensive; the second is that sponsors often have to account for all investments and recovering or paying underspends back into their investment accounts can be problematic. In this respect, underestimating the costs and having a contingency plan to make up a shortfall might be preferable, although you need to be mindful of running the risk of compromising the quality of the project if you can't make up the shortfall.

We used to reckon that if we could get within 10 per cent either way of our estimated costs, then we'd done okay. We felt that if we could stay within this parameter, we could always find items to buy that would give added value to the project if we were heading towards an underspend. If on the other hand we were heading towards an overspend, we could always find things to cut out of the venture that would not compromise its quality or chance of success.

By now, you may be thinking that estimating isn't an exact science. There are of course trained estimators who earn a reputation, and a good living, out of making cost estimations that are spot on. You may be lucky and have such a person in your team (if you do have such a person then look after them and hire them out to other schools). The likelihood, however, is that your projections may be based more on guesstimates than estimates. Don't be too concerned if this is the case because most estimates are wrong: right from the company involved in the Wembley project to the local builders who did my kitchen, my estimate is that well over 90 per cent of all estimates are wrong (I guess that I have a 10 per cent chance that this is correct). If you think about it, this makes sense. When estimates are made, not all of the facts are known. Most will only become apparent as the detailed work on the project starts to unfurl (use this as an excuse if your estimates are way off). So, how can we make a realistic calculation of costs?

Contrary to popular belief, the main costs of any project are not likely to be expensive items of equipment such as computers but the time taken by the project team to complete essential tasks. This is particularly true in education where staffing costs are estimated at 65 per cent of the overall costs. In this respect, we would describe a task as something that must be done before the next stage of the project can be undertaken.

The trick therefore is to break the estimate down into three key questions:

- How many tasks are necessary to complete the project?
- How much time and effort are required to complete a task?
- How long will it take to complete the task?

Here are five steps to help you build a clear picture of likely costs:

- Take time to understand the effort required for each task, how much staff time will have to be devoted to the task and how long it will take to complete it.
- Use your experience of working on similar projects to work out the likely effort and duration of each task. If you haven't experienced a project like this before, then talk to people who have. If you are struggling to find anyone who can help, then look for any published material or websites where you can find information to help.
- Determine who will have to work on the task. The costs associated with senior staff involvement will be higher than for more junior members of staff. If you need to bring in expertise from outside the project team to complete a task, make sure that you know how much this is likely to cost.
- Appreciate that two heads are better than one. Getting someone else's views on your estimates can't do any harm. You can always reject their suggestions but they may be able to contribute something that you had missed.
- Remember that estimating is not just a one-off process that is cast in stone at the beginning of the project. It is a formative process that is visited frequently throughout the life of the project. As we get further into the project and details become clearer, we need to revise our estimates.

If you have to re-estimate, then make sure that you let whoever is supporting the project know what's happening. Most project funders will understand if you need to move money between budget headings, although most don't like it when you move money from capital to revenue allocations. Very few will be forgiving if, at the end of the project, it comes to light that your actual spend on items bears very little similarity to what you projected.

A useful tool to have in this process is the project evaluation and review technique (PERT). PERT was devised in 1958 for the POLARIS missile project by the Program Evaluation Branch of the Special Projects office of the US Navy. To use PERT, you need three estimates of the time that it could take to complete a task:

- T(m): The most likely estimate of time to complete the activity.
- T(o): The most optimistic estimate of time to complete the activity.
- T(p): The most pessimistic estimate of time to complete the activity.

You then factor these estimates into a formula to produce T(e): The most probable estimate of time. In normal circumstances this could be:

$$T(e) = \frac{T(o) + 4T(m) + T(p)}{6}$$

You can adjust this formula to take account of any special factors such as the dire consequences of failing to complete on time, in which case a pessimistic view may be appropriate and the formula could become:

$$T(e) = \frac{T(o) + 3T(m) + 2T(p)}{6}$$

As the consequences become more dire, the T(p) multiplier can be increased.

You can apply the principles of PERT to calculating the costs of each task. In order to do this you need to appreciate that all tasks will involve contributions from most staffing levels within the project team. These can be described as:

- C(h): The hourly rate of the contribution that higher level staff make to the task.
- C(m): The hourly rate of the contribution that middle level staff make to the task.
- C(l): The hourly rate of the contribution that junior level staff make to the task.

You then factor these estimates into a formula to produce C(e): The most probable estimate of the hourly cost of each task. In normal circumstances this could be:

$$C(e) = \frac{C(h) + 4C(m) + C(l)}{6}$$

You can adjust this formula to take account of any special factors such as the need for more higher level contributions and the formula could become:

$$C(e) = \frac{2C(h) + 3C(m) + C(l)}{6}$$

As the need for the contribution from higher level staff becomes more apparent, the C(h) multiplier can be increased.

If we express T(e) in hours and C(e) as the hourly rate, then T(e) × C(e) will provide you with an estimate of cost of completing a task.

Hot Tip: Break the project down into a series of key tasks. Allocate tasks to key personnel (team members or outside agencies). Calculate the costs of delivering the task. Add all of these up to give you a final estimate (be prepared to revise this as new information comes to light).

DIFFERENT COST TYPES

Once you have estimated how much the project is likely to cost, you need to devise a spreadsheet that will be made up of direct and indirect costs, with an amount assigned for a contingency reserve to deal with unexpected costs. These can be defined as follows:

Direct cost: These costs are easily attributed to the project and charged on an item-by-item basis. Examples are:

- Staff salaries
- Capital equipment
- Raw materials
- Consultants' fees
- Subsistence and travel

Indirect costs: These costs are for items which have a wider use in the organisation where the project is based and where only a proportion of their total cost is charged to the project. Examples are:

- Telephone charges
- Office space (rent)
- Office equipment
- Publishing/printing costs
- Company-wide insurance

Contingency reserve: this is where a buffer is added to projects (usually a percentage of the total project cost and time) to cover risk. This fund is used when encountering unexpected events during the project. You should adjust your contingency reserve to the risk level identified for the project (see the section on risk management). A routine, well-practised project will have a lower contingency reserve (of say 5–10 per cent) than a project breaking new ground (of say 10–15 per cent).

Once you have finalised your budget spreadsheet and your project starts, you should regularly check actual spending against your budget estimate. This will tell you whether the project is progressing as planned or corrective action is needed.

Hot Tip: Use a spreadsheet to keep a check on actual against projected spend.

The final word on managing budgets:

- If you haven't experienced preparing a budget before, then talk to people who have. If you are struggling to find anyone who can help, then look for any published material or websites where you can find information to help.
- Whichever budgeting approach you choose, spend time to create your budget, check it carefully, and review it often to make sure you stay on track.
- Use a spreadsheet to keep a check on actual against projected spend.
- Take time to understand the effort required for each task, how much staff time will have to be devoted to the task and how long it will take to complete it.
- Determine which members of staff will have to work on the task.
- If you need to bring in expertise from outside the project team to complete a task, make sure that you know how much this is likely to cost.
- Appreciate that two heads are better than one. Getting someone else's views on your estimates can't do any harm. You can always reject their suggestions but they may be able to contribute something that you had missed.
- Remember that estimating is not just a one-off process that is cast in stone at the beginning of the project. It is a formative process that is visited frequently throughout the life of the project.

11

MANAGING CHANGE

Whether it involves making amendments to the curriculum, revising a process or structure within your organisation or a human resource procedure, the work of leadership will have an element of bringing about change to it. An important part of the leader's role therefore is the ability to manage change and the capacity to realise that all change evokes the emotions of fear and embarrassment as well as those of excitement and anticipation.

Some changes are quite significant, such as developments in information technology (IT) that have created a world where people can communicate on a level they couldn't possibly have dreamed of less than a decade ago. A far cry from the young Computer Studies graduate of the 1970s who spurned a career in IT claiming computers were a 'flash in the pan' and there was no career to be had in computing (well, Bob was only 21 at the time). Other changes although less dramatic may still have an impact on people. We read somewhere about someone's panic reaction to the new automatic flushing toilet, thinking they had been followed into the cubicle.

Many people find change to be both painful and inconvenient, preferring to stay in their comfort zones or failing to understand the reasoning behind it. Each of us differ in the way we perceive change; what may be fresh and stimulating to one person may be a major disruption to another. We also differ in our abilities to face the unknown and deal with the uncertainty that change brings. We don't think that for one minute this section will deal with all of the issues that you face as someone going through or managing a change process. What it will do is give you a greater understanding of the issues that people face whilst going through change and some useful tools to help you manage a change programme.

Unlike some of the other sections in this book, finding which theorists to include was easy. Most of the process models for change start with Kurt Lewin and most of the effects of change models emanate from Elisabeth Kübler-Ross. These are our starting points.

A PROCESS MODEL

Kurt Lewin (1935) created the force field analysis (FFA) model as a social psychological tool (see Figure 11.1). It is now widely recognised as a major organisational change planning tool. FFA looks at the forces driving change forward and measures them against the forces resisting change. Like other aspects of Lewin's work the basic idea is simple – it is the application that gives it its true value. Although there are a number of variations, the basic process is:

Form the FFA team: Assemble a team of around four or five people to work with you on the force field.

Define the change proposal: This is best written in a box in the top centre of a sheet of paper with a vertical line drawn from the centre top to the centre bottom of the page.

Describe the drivers: List the forces for change in a column on the left-hand side (LHS) of the centre line.

Describe the resistors: List the forces opposing change in a column on the right-hand side (RHS) of the centre line.

Score the forces: Assign a score of say 1 (weak) to 5 (strong) to each of the forces, denoting their respective strengths. For added visual effect draw vertical arrows by each force towards the centre line representing the power of the force (the bolder the arrow, the greater the force).

As you start to add the drivers and resistors to the force field, ask some important questions around:

- What benefits the organisation will accrue from the change?
- Who are the supporters and opponents of change?
- What obstacles are there likely to be? What are the risks associated with these obstacles?

As you do this, identify as many important factors as you can – you can always score the less important ones low or take them out altogether from the force field.

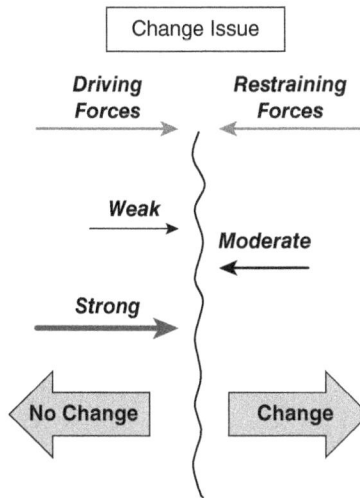

Figure 11.1 The force field model

Don't be fazed if you get the same issue acting as both a driver and a resistor. Remember that people's perceptions about what benefits or harms them will differ. You can always reconcile this once you begin the analysis. Please note here that when you come to score each of the forces, this may be entirely subjective. This is why I recommend that you involve others. You can either debate the strength of each force and try to reach a consensus, or take an average across the board.

Once you are satisfied that you have completed the FFA an initial glance should tell you whether change is a done deal (drivers far outweighing resistors), a dead duck (resistors far outweighing drivers) or a difficult decision (little to choose between the two). If you are committed to change, then you need to look at how you can either strengthen the forces or weaken the resistors and what effort needs to go into this to have a stronger LHS of the force field.

Don't underestimate the amount of effort it will take to do this properly. Try it out on a few personal change issues or some less important work-based ones. Be certain that you are confident with the approach before tackling something that has greater significance to the organisation. Remember, the organisation isn't defined by bricks and mortar – it is defined by the people that work there. They will be more affected by change. It's important therefore that you appreciate the effects that change may have on them.

Take it from us, this is a really powerful process model that, if used correctly, will help you in many personal as well as professional decisions concerning the feasibility of making changes. What you also need to consider is the effect that change will have on the people who have a stake in the project.

CASE STUDY

Due to its success Karen's school had to expand to satisfy the demand for pupil places. However, not all the fruits of the school's success were palatable ones. Some difficult decisions had to be taken, not least of which, due to the size of the cohorts, was the organisation of pupils. The more she thought about it the more attractive the option of accommodating pupils in mixed age classes appeared. Karen knew that there would be a storm of protest from all quarters once she proposed doing this, despite a growing conviction that this was in the best interests of pupils. In order to reconcile what needed to be done, Karen invited representatives from the governors, parents and teachers and learners to present what they felt were the factors in favour or against organising pupils into mixed age groups.

Armed with this intelligence, she drew up an FFA, agreeing beforehand with stakeholders certain key considerations which could: have a serious impact on the budget; be detrimental to the health, welfare and safety of pupils; hinder pupil achievement; and be given agreed weightings to reflect their relative importance.

This turned out to be critical, for on a simple calculation of points for and points against, the proposal would not have been adopted. However, taking account of weightings the proposal won the day, and although a number of individuals remained lukewarm, as a result of the transparency of the decision-making process they could appreciate the arguments for and against and the reason for the final decision. As a result they were prepared, in the words of one governor, 'to give it a go'.

Hot Tip: Represent graphically all of the factors that are driving and resisting change. Once you have a clear picture of this, deciding what needs to be done is less complicated.

AN EFFECT OF CHANGE MODEL

Elisabeth Kübler-Ross (2005) challenged beliefs that traumatic events should be 'swept under the carpet'. Her five-stage model was originally intended to help people deal with bereavement but has since been the catalyst for many adaptations and extensions relating to change management. The five stages are shown in Figure 11.2. The stages in this model can be summarised as:

Denial: This is the initial stage of numbness and shock provoking a sense of disbelief. It can be either a conscious or an unconscious refusal to accept what is happening. People stuck in this stage may think that the people responsible for the project will begin to think it's a bad idea and it may just go away.

Anger: When acceptance of the reality of the situation takes place, denial turns to anger, either through self-recrimination or anger with others. This may result in attempts to sabotage as they try to undermine the project or prevent it from happening.

Bargaining: This takes place to seek to get modifications to the project and a resolution. A compromise may not be the ideal solution but may stave off the next stage.

Depression: This is the stage reached if bargaining has failed and the reality of the situation sets in. It's natural that emotions such as sadness or regret at any loss will be felt. This stage is necessary to demonstrate acceptance of the reality of the situation.

Acceptance: Dealing with sadness and regret is a necessary prerequisite for acceptance. Acceptance is reached once the individual realises that resisting the change is not going to make it go away or that the new project will actually work.

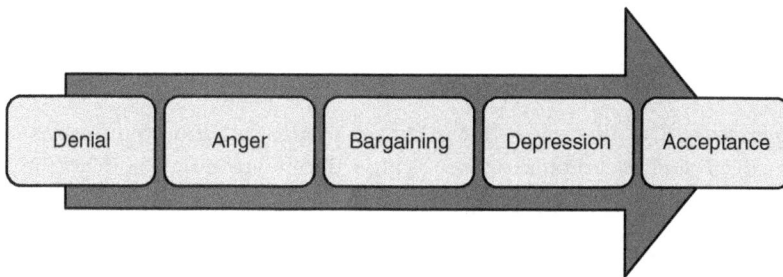

Figure 11.2   **The grief model**

Kübler-Ross advises us that people don't move through the stages in a well-ordered sequential manner and that regression may be an essential part of the process before the ultimate state of acceptance is reached. She also warns us that some people may get stuck in one stage for an uncomfortable period of time. As a school leader you need to be aware of this and recognise that not everyone is going to embrace your vision of what the new change will achieve.

Involve stakeholders in discussions about the need for the change and what impact this is likely to have. Canvass their ideas about what needs to be done and how the change should be carried out. It's not essential that you accept all of their suggestions; the mere act of listening and explaining the need for change will build trust between you and the individuals involved.

Establish as many lines of communication with the staff as possible. Don't restrict these opportunities to formal meetings. Get out of your office and talk to people, listen to their concerns and answer their questions as fully as you can. It's better to say 'I don't have an answer to that question, but I'll find out and get back to you' than to try to bluff your way out of the problem. People follow leaders they trust.

An elaboration of Kübler-Ross's ideas is **John Fisher's** (2012) transition curve. Fisher argues that how an organisation deals with change depends on who initiated the idea for the change and what control they have over this. He suggests that no matter how small the change, it has the potential to have a major impact on certain individuals within the organisation, their self-view and subsequent performance. He describes this impact in terms of a series of transitional events that can be summarised as:

Anxiety and confusion: The awareness that some events that happen within the school lie outside of your control.

Happiness: The awareness that your feelings over these events are shared by your colleagues.

Fear: The awareness that change resulting from the project is imminent. This could lead to your lack of acceptance of any change and denial.

Threat: The awareness that change will impact on your core behaviour.

Guilt: The awareness that your past behaviour was questionable. This could lead to awareness that your beliefs and values are incompatible with those of the school and a sense of disillusionment or defeat.

Depression: The awareness that a lack of motivation and confusion is setting in. This could lead to a failure to see where things are going and hostility with or from others.

Gradual acceptance: The awareness that you need to do something positive in order to start moving forward.

Fisher warns of the conflicts that people may face when challenging their existing values and beliefs and whether these are compatible with those of the project, and the subsequent dangers of getting too engrossed in the emotion of the change.

As a school leader, in order to help individuals and organisations to move through the transition effectively you need to understand their perception of the past present and future. You need to ask: 'What were their past experiences of change? How did they cope with this? What will they be losing or gaining as a result of the change?' You may not be able to change this perception, so concentrate your efforts on supporting them to work through the implications for themselves. Encourage them to reflect on why they are feeling the way they are.

Don't think that change needs to be a dramatic or frequently occurring event. When **Pedlar et al.** published the first edition of their influential work on the learning organisation in 1991, they spawned a generation of public and private sector bodies, including schools, wanting to be recognised as learning organisations.

The principles underpinning the notion of learning organisations were founded on the belief that such an organisation needed to change constantly to meet the needs of its customers and clients. When the authors published the second edition of the book in 1997, they admitted that their principles were essentially flawed, and that the idea that change needed to be constant was a potential recipe for chaos and disaster within an organisation. They suggested that the word *constantly* in their definition should be replaced with *consciously*, implying that in order to be effective, the organisation needed to have an awareness of where it was and a willingness or desire to want the change. They also suggested that change needed to be incremental with periods of consolidation – a series of steps rather than a continuous curve.

CASE STUDY

Dee patiently listened to Eddie's complaints about the failure of his team to respond positively to his proposals for curriculum change. After making him a coffee and opening the biscuit tin, she reminded Eddie of his recent response to a DfE initiative. Even as he responded how that was different, Eddie knew what Dee was driving at. His objections to the DfE proposals had been based on deeply held educational principals so it was not inconceivable that his team also held deep convictions, which even if different to his could be valid. Also if some objections to Eddie's proposals were of a more personal nature, Dee subtly steered him to admit that there was a less altruistic issue contributing to his own objections at the time.

Ten minutes and a few biscuits later Eddie felt more positive about the situation. His proposed changes were valid and their implementation was necessary, but he realised that he had failed to take account of the perceptions of those who were integral to the success of the project. A good deal of discussion, compromise and persuasion, not to mention some helpings of 'humble-pie', were needed to win staff over. Eddie resolved that next time change was proposed a greater degree of preparation, awareness and sensitivity would be needed to ensure a more positive reaction at the outset.

When John Heywood wrote in the mid-16th century that 'A rolling stone gathers no moss', he was suggesting that nothing sticks if you fail to pause occasionally and take stock. In terms of managing change, this emphasises the need to consolidate after each episode of change before moving on to the next episode. A point that was emphasised some 300 years later by Alphonse Karr who wrote, *'Plus ca change, plus c'est la meme chose'* (roughly translated as 'The more things change, the more they stay the same').

Michael Barber was Chief Adviser to the Secretary of State for Education in the UK from 1997–2001 and founder of the US Education Delivery Institute. Working alongside **Andy Moffit** and **Paul Kihn** at the consultancy group McKinsey, he developed a model for organisational leaders to ensure educational organisations respond better to the need for change in how they deliver learning. Barber et al. (2010) referred to the model as *deliverology*, which they described as a systematic process for driving progress and delivering results in government and the public sector.

The model is based on five principles, which can be summarised as:

Develop a foundation for delivering change: The key stages here are: to define an aspiration; to review the current state of delivery; to build the new delivery unit; and to establish a guiding coalition that can remove barriers to change, influence and support the unit's work at crucial moments and provide counselling and advice.

Understand the delivery challenge: In this stage it's important to evaluate past and present performance and understand the drivers of performance and relevant systems activities.

Plan for delivery: This is where the reform strategy must be determined, targets and trajectories are set and delivery plans produced.

Drive delivery forward: This is done by establishing the routines to drive and monitor performance, to solve problems early and rigorously and sustain and build momentum.

Create an irreversible delivery culture: The final stage involves building the system's capacity and communicating the delivery message.

Barber et al. argue that at the core of deliverology is the need for effective relationship-building; what the authors describe as 'unleashing the alchemy of relationships'. Here are some key questions to ask in order to help achieve this:

- What is it the organisation wants to achieve? Where do they currently perceive themselves to be? What do they need to do to get to where they want to be? Once these questions have been answered, set about getting a commitment to action to achieve the aspiration.
- What do we know about how the organisation has performed in the past? Is the evidence we have on past performance reliable, relevant and valid? Do we understand what's causing under-achievement? Are we capable of dealing with this? Once these questions have been answered, identify the people who can make a change.
- What are the barriers that the organisation has put up to resist change? Accept that change may take time. You may need to identify the factors that are influencing the organisation to be resistant to change. Organisational and individual planning is vital and will need constant reflection, revision, reworking and realistic support.
- How much time and energy can we devote to support the organisation to change? Accept that the barriers and problems affecting change are real for the organisation and you need to have an appreciation of the severity of the problem and how important the organisation considers the solution to be. If both of these factors are significant, then persist in addressing them.
- Once you have the organisation thinking positively about change, don't allow the momentum to stall. Make sure you let everyone know about what's been achieved and the efforts made to get there.

Change should be considered a process rather than a product or, if you prefer, a journey rather than a destination. It's important that organisational leaders, managers, teachers and learners pause to reflect and consider where they are on the journey. In this respect, the cornerstone of change is all stakeholders thinking about their role, their impact, their successes, their failures and their efforts.

CASE STUDY

Simon was something of a railway enthusiast, which explained the model that he used to in order to get staff to invest in change.

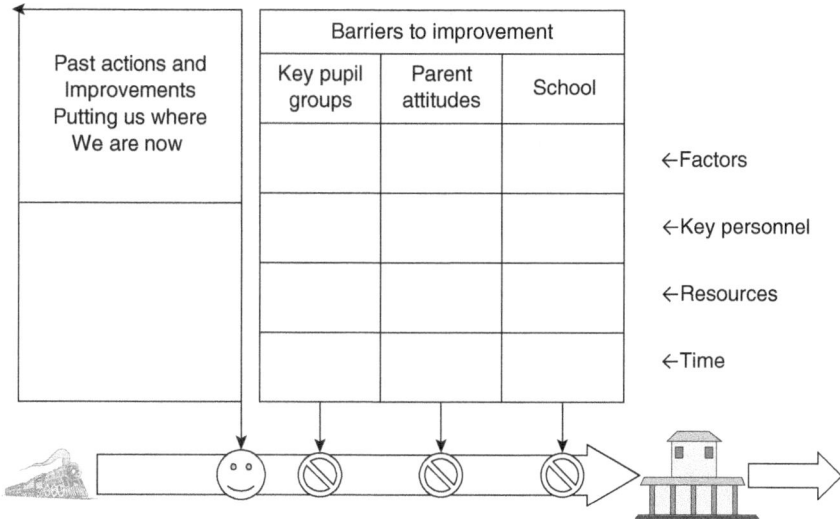

Past actions and Improvements Putting us where We are now	Barriers to improvement			
	Key pupil groups	Parent attitudes	School	
				←Factors
				←Key personnel
				←Resources
				←Time

Question: What/where can you contribute to the school achieving its next 'destination'?

It illustrated that the school was on a journey of improvement; the stations represented targets and destinations on the journey. The journey to improvement was plotted on the diagram for all to contribute to and see what was required and by whom. Most importantly was the question posed to each individual member of staff about their personal contribution to the project. Staff were happy to go along for the ride!

Hot Tip: Accept that change is a process, not a product. Never ignore the impact that this process has on people.

The final word on managing change:

- Accept that change is a process, not a product.
- Ascertain what is it the organisation wants to achieve.
- Analyse what you know about how the organisation has performed in the past.
- Be certain that the evidence we have on past performance is reliable, relevant and valid, and that you understand what's causing under-achievement.
- Make sure that you are capable of dealing with this.
- Identify the people who can make a change and deal with any opposition that you encounter.
- Decide how much time and energy you can devote to support the organisation to change.
- Accept that the barriers and problems affecting change are real for the organisation, and you need to have an appreciation of the severity of the problem and how important the organisation considers the solution to be.
- Once you have the organisation thinking positively about change, don't allow the momentum to stall.
- Make sure you let everyone know about what's been achieved and the efforts made to get there.
- Never ignore the impact that this process has on people.

12

STAKEHOLDERS

A stakeholder is any individual or organisation who has an interest in the success of the school. These will vary from those who have a direct impact on the management of the school, such as the staff and governors, to those who benefit directly from the success of the establishment, such as the learners and their parents. There are many other stakeholders whose contributions towards the establishment and rewards accruing from its success are less direct and tangible. These may include suppliers, employers and the wider local community.

All stakeholders, by their very nature, will have a vested interest in the school succeeding and will exert some influence in order to make this happen. The level of interest, however, and the influence that they exert will vary considerably. As the school leader you need tools for handling both the straightforward stakeholder issues and the more complex ones that may require a less conventional approach.

Gerry Johnson and **Kevin Scholes** (2002) argue that mapping project stakeholders is an excellent project management tool which identifies and assesses the effect of different individuals or groups of stakeholders on the school. Using a chess analogy, Figure 12.1 is our interpretation of their levels of interest and power within the organisation.

In this model, stakeholders are recorded on a matrix which plots their level of interest in issues that affect the project against the power they possess to exercise those interests. The stakeholders in this way are broadly divided into four groups:

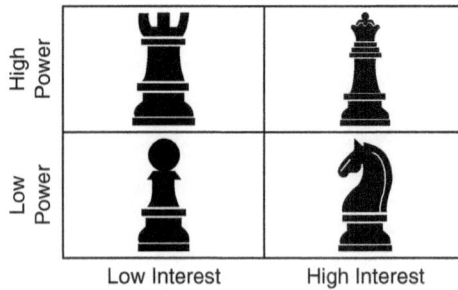

Figure 12.1 The Bates' stakeholder chess model

The **Pawns**: You can ignore these as they pose little threat to your leadership unless they start to gang up on you. Some pawns (such as irate parents) have the potential to creep up on you and become major influences (such as parent governors). Keep an eye on these.

The **Knights**: These may be important in some of the more minor developments within the school so keep them informed about what's going on with these developments and make good use of their contributions. Although some knights (such as the school caretaker) may not be considered to be as powerful as rooks and queens, they do have a capacity for making surprise moves that may unsettle you.

The **Rooks**: These are major players (such as governors) in any undertaking. Don't take them for granted, but don't get too concerned about them until you need them to play an active role when the high power they wield in the running of the school may be crucial to the undertaking. Don't be fazed if they remain dormant for long phases, as more often than not they will have a major role to play at some stage.

The **Queens**: These are the members of your staff and senior management team. You must keep these people satisfied as they hold the key to the school's success. Lose them early on in any undertaking with little or no gain and you might as well pack it in.

Use the above information to map and analyse the different groups of stakeholder according to their level of interest and power in the project. Then set about making yourself known to them and winning their confidence. Talk to them and get to know how they feel about you and your work. Find out what's likely to motivate them to either support or oppose you and what they expect from you.

Dealing with stakeholders may not always be a straightforward case of winning their confidence by simply by talking to them. There will be stakeholders whose agenda may not be clear. Some will oppose the project, some will support it and others will either be uncertain of the project or your capacity to deliver it. **Gerard Egan** (1994) categorises these stakeholders as follows:

Partners: Those who support your endeavours.

Allies: Those who, if encouraged sufficiently, will support you.

Fellow Travellers: Those who support your ideas, but not necessarily you.

Fence-sitters: Those whose allegiances are not clear.

Loose Cannons: Those about whom you have no idea which way they will turn.

Opponents: Those who oppose your ideas, but have nothing against you personally.

Adversaries: Those who oppose you and your ideas.

Bedfellows: Those who support your ideas in principle, but may not trust you.

Voiceless: Those who have little or no power to support or oppose you or your ideas.

CASE STUDY

Craig, the site manager of a secondary academy, as considered himself to be the vital cog in the everyday running of the school: headteacher, Marcia's judgement was somewhat more qualified. Superficially there was little wrong with their relationship, and Craig could appear to be anxious to please, particularly in dealing with matters of personal concern to Marcia herself. However, it was hard to avoid drawing the conclusion that what you saw was not always what you got. Craig had his own priorities and these did not always match Marcia's: his appeared to be of a more practical, even personal nature, whilst hers revolved around pupils' education, welfare and safety.

Craig was very personable and readily engaged socially with staff, governors, parents, members of the community and visitors. Ever eager to obtain information, he would pass it on if he thought it would enhance his status or belittle those with whom he had an issue at the time. Such information would frequently be given a twist, either deliberately or due to an inadequate understanding of the facts he had garnered.

Marcia had to be mindful therefore in her conversations with Craig and ensure that the staff were similarly on their guard in not providing information, which could, when repeated or embellished, create unfavourable impressions of the school and of individuals working within it. At the same time she developed a strategy where every realistic opportunity was taken to involve and consult Craig, flattering his sense of his own self-importance rather than stimulating his antagonism. The former meant that in publicising, or exaggerating, his own contributions to initiatives and so on, recipients were at least receiving positive messages about the school.

When Craig moved on to a bigger and in his words 'better' school, Marcia's involvement strategy was hugely successful with his replacement Julia, who wholeheartedly embraced being consulted and as a consequence volunteered to use her considerable skills to undertake numerous projects of real benefit to the school, such as constructing elaborate classroom props for projects, creating a garden and maintaining it in lunch hours and after school with the help of pupils.

Egan describes working on the 'shadow side' as a tactic for dealing with those stakeholders who cannot be dealt with using conventional management practices. Partners and allies, for example, need to be kept on side, whereas opponents and adversaries may have to be discredited and marginalised. Fence-sitters and the voiceless have to be seduced to ensure they don't go over to the other side.

CASE STUDY

Faced with an increase in pupil numbers Sumaya came to the conclusion, after studying a number of options, that one of the phases within the school should be organised on the basis of mixed-age classes. Despite setting out the reasons for this there was strong opposition among some parents, staff and governors of the school. Sumaya had expected this, but anticipated that the opposition would subside when the system was up and running and seen to be a success.

What she had failed to appreciate were the agenda and actions of a parent who also happened to be a governor and who chose their moment to strike when Sumaya was 140 miles away from the school on a residential visit with a group of pupils. This involved holding clandestine meetings with other governors, inciting parents and unsettling staff. On her return to school Sumaya was confronted with a difficult situation: a chair of governors adopting an ambivalent position, a group of disgruntled parents and a small number of staff gloating because they had 'told her so'.

It's fair to say that she dealt with this by using a fair degree of chicanery which enabled the planned organisational changes to go ahead and led to the parent-governor resigning her position and removing her child from the school. In addition from a group of parents, who overtly supported Sumaya, there emerged a diligent and supportive parents association.

When later reflecting on the incident, Sumaya would rehearse a scenario that could well have pre-empted what could have been a very damaging episode for the school as well as her career.

Hot Tip: Recognise that without some political savvy, you'll get checkmated by those stakeholders who play the game better than you.

A final word on managing stakeholders:

- Identify and get to know the key stakeholders in your organisation. Work out what power, influence and interests each stakeholder has.
- Identify those stakeholders that might have an impact on your school plan. Rank them in terms of possible impact.
- Keep a watchful eye on those stakeholders with little power and little interest, but don't waste too much time communicating with them.
- Talk to the ones with little power but high interest. They may lack the power to influence decisions, but may be useful when it comes to working up the detail on your school plan or convincing other stakeholders.
- Put just enough effort into the ones with high power but little interest to keep them satisfied, but accept they may not want to get involved in the detail of the plan.
- Focus your attention on the ones with high power and high interest. These are the people you need to fully engage with to get the job done.
- Continue to keep a watchful eye on the others and brief them regularly, but remember where your priorities lie.
- Get to know what each stakeholder feels about your change agenda and you personally.
- Socialising with people you don't particularly like may be a chore, but the odd drink outside of work may save hours of work in the office and at formal meetings.
- In focusing on dealing with those that you consider *opponents* and *adversaries*, don't lose sight of the importance of consolidating your *partners* and *allies*.
- Pay attention to the *undecideds*; if they suddenly side with the *opposition* it could prove disastrous for you.

13

CULTURE

Throughout this book, we've looked at key factors in the process of leadership and management that you have a reasonable level of control over. These include the staff, systems, operations and your own management skills. It is equally important to consider factors that you have less or no control over at all. One such factor is the culture of the organisation that you work for and the impact this can have as you try to develop the organisation.

Lee Bolman and **Terence Deal** (2008) discuss the long-standing controversy over the relationship between culture and leadership. They ask if leaders shape the culture of the organisation or are shaped by it. Before trying to unravel this question, it's important to get a grip on what we mean by culture and the type of cultures that may exist within an organisation.

A group of management students were once asked what they understood by the word 'culture'. The answers ranged from 'religious beliefs' through to 'the thing that grows in the bottom of your cup if you forget to wash it when you leave the staffroom on Friday'. Although their tutor was looking for a response along the lines of **Edgar Schein**'s (1985) definition, 'A pattern of shared basic assumptions invented, discovered, or developed by a given group as it learns to cope with its problems of external adaptation and internal integration', he acknowledged each contribution with comments such as 'Values and beliefs certainly impact on culture' and 'Like the blobby bits in your unwashed cup on a Monday morning, culture is an organic process in which the end product can have both a harmful or healing effect' (we're not sure that penicillin was quite discovered in this way though). The range of student responses demonstrates the complexity of the subject. A popular way of describing organisational culture is to use the iceberg analogy shown in Figure 13.1.

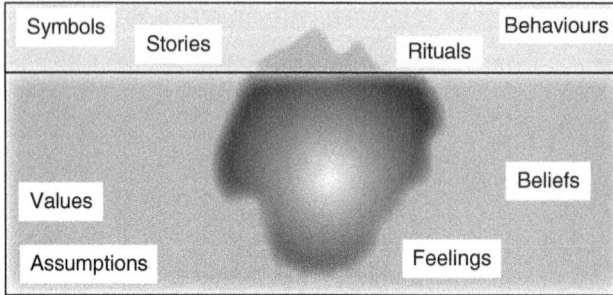

Figure 13.1   The iceberg culture model

In this analogy, things such as symbols, stories, rituals and behaviours are the factors that appear above the surface and are obvious to many, whereas values, beliefs, feelings and assumptions are the factors that are below the surface and hidden to many.

Although organisational cultures vary widely from one organisation to the next, commonalities do exist and organisational cultures can generally be categorised into something that an organisation *is* (the image people have of how the organisation goes about its business) or something that an organisation *has* (its fundamental values and beliefs). The two entries that follow contain one in each of these categories.

We're going to deal first with a theory on culture that depicts how an organisation is defined, in terms of its image. **Charles Handy** (2011) suggests that the metaphor of Greek gods can be a useful way of depicting the personalities that influence how an organisation is perceived both internally and externally. These can be matrixed in terms of: 'supportive/directive' and 'concern for others/self-interest' (see Figure 13.2).

The characteristics of each of the gods can be summarised as:

- **Zeus**: (Web culture) Power is concentrated in the hands of one individual. Leaders are power driven, strong and charismatic. The organisation is driven by hard-and-fast rules with little scope for flexibility or interaction between staff. A spider's web is used by Handy to portray this culture. If the spider or source of power dies, then the future of the organisation becomes questionable.
- **Apollo**: (Role culture) Power is hierarchical and defined in the roles people fulfil. Leaders are well-ordered and predicable, logical and analytical. There is a reliance on mutual respect for the role holders' positions throughout the organisation. Handy uses a Greek temple to describe this culture. Each pillar of the temple represents a key role. If one of the pillars (or roles) no longer functions, then the temple (or organisation) begins to shake.

- **Athena**: (Task culture) Power is derived from the cooperation required to complete tasks. Leaders are wise, ambitious and good at solving problems. A *net* is used to represent this culture. The net is a series of linked operations, each fulfilling a specific responsibility. If one of the links is broken the net begins to lose effectiveness.
- **Dionysus**: (Existential culture) Power is with the individuals within the organisation. Leaders are self-interested and hard to influence. Stars in the firmament portray this culture. It's based on individuals whose allegiance to the organisational is overridden by their own individual needs.

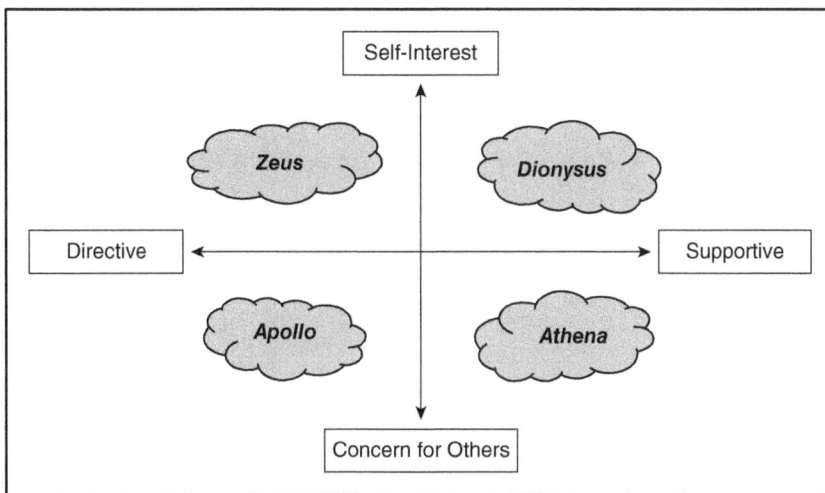

Figure 13.2   The management gods model

Handy argues that, although an organisation may have a mixture of cultures, there will likely be one dominant culture. He also claims that factors such as the size of the organisation, production mode and how long the organisation has been in business will determine which type of culture will be the dominant one.

Use Handy's questionnaire in his book, *The Gods of Management* (2011), to identify what type of culture best describes your organisation and what type of culture you function best in as a leader. Getting others to do the questionnaire will give you an idea of any possible mismatch between what your organisation wants and what the people working there want.

If questionnaires or metaphors aren't your cup of tea, talk to people both inside and outside of your school about how they view the school. Remember they may not have read Handy so avoid using the metaphors and try to get a feel for if they think the power in the school is centralised around one person (Zeus), *or* does it put the emphasis on order and efficiency that relies upon the already established routines (Apollo), *or* does it distribute power to staff based upon their ability to perform the task necessary at a given time (Athena), *or* is the focus of the school built on the success of individuals, rather than the school (Dionysus).

Of course we can't resist the temptation of asking the age-old question 'What is the difference between God and a Headteacher?' The answer, of course (with apologies to the profession), is 'God doesn't think he's a Headteacher'.

Carl Steinhoff and **Robert Owens** (1989) developed four metaphors (Family, Machine, Circus and Little Shop of Horrors), which they refer to as *phenotypes*, that characterise the cultures which may exist in organisations. Figure 13.3 depicts these cultures, which we have categorised in terms of *chaos* or *control* and *collective* or *individual*.

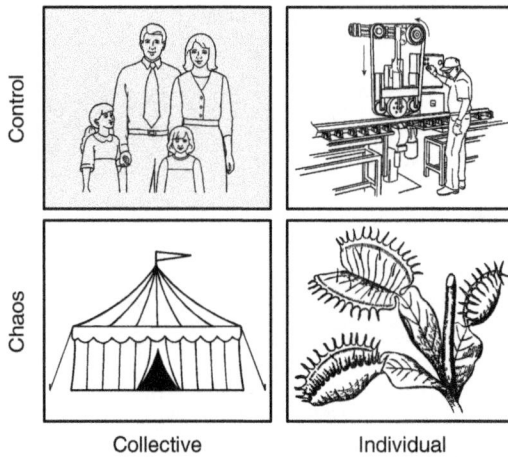

Figure 13.3   The phenotype model

We have adapted the metaphors to show how extremes can exist in each category:

The Family: The school is viewed in terms of the relationships that exist there. They could be a cosy and close-knit family like the *Waltons* or a dysfunctional one like the *Simpsons*.

The Machinist: The school is viewed purely in terms of a production line. This could be a well-oiled company, producing products of quality such as Rolls-Royce (a car synonymous with the word 'quality') or the company that made the Trabant (described in one car magazine as a 'hollow lie of a car constructed of recycled worthlessness').

The Circus: The school is viewed in terms of the artistic and intellectual quality of its staff. Heads are viewed as the *masters-of-ceremony* (keeping a watchful eye on performers) or *show-stealers* (placing their artistic ability above that of the other performers.

The Little Shop of Horrors: The school is viewed in terms of its unpredictability and chaotic nature. Organisations in this culture either have a *Napoleonic* complex (that promotes dominance and control) or *Jekyll and Hyde* personalities (that promote uncertainty and chaos).

We suspect that some readers don't share our passion for using metaphors to make sense of, and analyse, what's going on in an organisation. Certainly viewing education in terms of a production line will rest uneasy with many. But what is the popular view of education if it's not taking in raw materials (the learners), putting them through a transformation process (the teaching) and producing finished articles with added value? This is depicted in Figure 13.4.

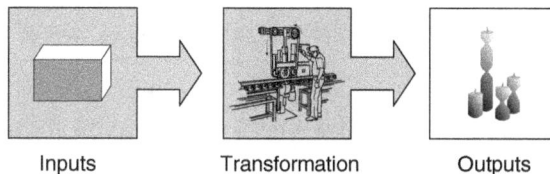

| Inputs | Transformation | Outputs |

Figure 13.4   **The transformation process model**

Of course we need to rationalise the transformation model to take account of the fact that in education not all inputs (learners) come in homogeneous lumps of 3x2, not everyone goes through the transformation process at the same rate and not everyone achieves the same results.

Although we've use Steinhoff and Owens in this entry, there is a whole raft of great metaphors out there. **Gareth Morgan** (2006), in particular, offers some great organisational metaphors in *Images of Organisations*. I suspect that we were taken by their use of the *Little Shop of Horrors* and the image that one of us had of a college principal that he once worked with as a blood-sucking, flesh-eating plant. But that's another story ...

Once you have a picture of what you and others think the overriding organisational culture is, consider the following: What attributes would a leader need to be successful in this culture? To what extent do you display those attributes? Can you identify a successful leader within your organisation (or outside if none are readily available) and ask to what extent they display the attributes that are best suited to the culture of your organisation? Start modelling your behaviours on what they do. Be aware that making decisions about changing the culture of your organisation may not be popular with everyone. We can learn a lot about changing the culture by looking outside the educational spectrum.

CASE STUDY

The owner of the local football club that we have both supported for over fifty years wanted to use a large slice of the club's finances to build a new stand that would allow him to erect an advertising hoarding on the outside of the stand (which happened to face a busy stretch of motorway) that would bring in revenue from selling advertising space. Many of the club's supporters wanted to see the money used to buy new players.

Had the club not changed the culture from a football team that makes money to a business venture that sustains a football team then we are certain the town would no longer have a team playing in the football league. We are grateful for the owner's vision but we wish we'd win a few more games.

John West-Burnham and **Dave Harris** (2015) offer an interesting perspective on culture within the context of education. They discuss school cultures as being any of the following:

- **Bureaucratic**, where there is a real boss and things being done in a set way. In this culture, the school is driven by rules with little scope for flexibility or interaction between peers.
- **Collegial**, where there is a reliance on mutual trust throughout the organisation. In this culture the emphasis is with networks rather than individuals. Decision-making is shared by staff and students.
- **Toxic**, where there is a sense of negativity to most things, a focus on failure and a resistance to want to change. Staff are reluctant to share ideas, materials or solutions.

There is a series of questionnaires provided by West-Burnham and Harris to enable you to measure the culture in the school from the point of view of leaders, staff, pupils and visitors to the school.

CASE STUDY

Here are the cultural values that appear in the booklet for an outstanding adult education college:

'We work with partners who share our values and give equally to support our learners and the community. We celebrate diversity, individuality and difference, valuing the richness this brings and we respect others and we challenge any form of discrimination. We own our decisions, taking responsibility for the consequences of our actions, we keep our promises and we resist apportioning blame when things don't go as planned.'

Bold words indeed! We'd certainly want our grandchildren to be students at this college. Is this typical, however, of the culture of this college? At what point do people stop looking at it through rose-tinted glasses and using glib rhetoric in their promotional literature? Is it when you find the college is 200 yards from the nearest bus stop in a run-down area of the town? Maybe it's when you wander through the prison-type railings that protect the college from intruders? Could it be when the uniformed security guard asks to see your pass? Or is the mutterings you hear from staff about a lack of resources? Or when you hear that staff absences are at an all-time high?

Yes, we know that there are safeguarding issues that protect learners from evil influences, and that there are excellent schools operating in run-down areas, but the culture within your organisation shouldn't be defined by what appears in the promotional booklets or is proudly displayed on the walls of the organisation but the attitudes, behaviour and ethos of the organisation.

> **Hot Tip**: Use Burnham-West and Harris's questionnaires (available on a CD-Rom as part of their work on school leadership) to measure a multitude of views taken from a range of sources.

Take a look at the case study from industry below and then at the question that follows:

CASE STUDY

Steve Jobs, alongside Steve Wozniak, was the co-founder of Apple Computers. He is credited with revolutionising the computer industry by making smaller, cheaper, easier to understand equipment that was more accessible to everyday consumers. Not actually having had an official title with the company he co-founded, Jobs was pushed into a more marginalised position and thus left Apple in 1985 to begin a new hardware and software enterprise called NeXT. Due to him taking a series of risks on the availability of operating systems, NeXT floundered. The following year he returned to his post as Apple's CEO.

Not all of Jobs's ventures failed during his time away from Apple. He purchased an animation company which later became Pixar Animation Studios. Believing in Pixar's potential, Jobs initially invested US$50 million of his own money in the company. The studio went on to produce wildly popular movies such as *Toy Story*, *Finding Nemo* and *The Incredibles*; Pixar's films have collectively netted US$4 billion. The studio merged with Walt Disney in 2006, making Steve Jobs Disney's largest shareholder.

Where would you locate Steve Jobs and Apple in the categories provided by Charles Handy, Steinhoff and Owens and Burnham-West and Harris?

Once you've done this, work out where the gaps are between where your organisation is as a culture and where you should be in terms of leadership. Use a force field analysis (see Chapter 11) to help you to identify what factors are driving you towards being where you want to be with changing the culture and those that are in the organisation's way of doing things and resisting forward momentum.

Once you have established where you are in terms of the culture and where you want to be, don't mess around; be decisive and devise an action plan to close the gaps. Use the SMARTER model (see Chapter 14) to help you plan.

In this chapter, we have tried to avoid getting too bogged down in debating the issue of whether culture is something the organisation *is* or whether it is something the organisation *has*. It is, however, important that you understand how you are perceived by the outside world. How often have you heard it said that 'We can't work with this organisation or this head teacher/principal because they can't change their ways'?

If culture is something that the organisation *is* (i.e. it has characteristics that are ingrained), it may be more difficult to change than if it is something the organisation *has* (i.e. a set of beliefs). Alan Sugar and Simon Cowell will never be looked on as nice guys because it may not suit the businesses that have grown up around them for them to be seen in this light. Both would struggle to make it in the world of public service – after all, who would want to see an outspoken and occasionally obnoxious host of a show like *The Apprentice* have a prominent role in public service or politics? Anita Roddick, on the other hand, changed people's perceptions of The Body Shop from just another high street retailer selling hair and skin products to being at the retailer's forefront of protecting the environment.

Whatever standpoint you take on this, if you want your organisation to give their absolute support to your leadership then you need to be certain that you have clearly thought through the following:

- What is the existing culture in the organisation?
- What culture does there needs to be for my leadership to flourish?
- How you can make the necessary changes to either the culture within the organisation or your leadership style?

It might be that you may not consider you need to change anything about your leadership style. Remember the story of the proud mother at her son's passing out parade in the Army, exclaiming that everyone was out of step except her son? Well, maybe they were – maybe it's the organisation that needs to change to match your leadership, but can you afford to be complacent about this? The old adage 'If it ain't broke, don't fix it' may be okay if you are content with mediocrity, but if you want to be an outstanding leader then replace it with 'Have a closer look, you may be missing something that needs fixing'.

Here's another quick look at an example from the commercial world:

CASE STUDY

In just fifteen years, Enron grew from nowhere to become America's seventh largest company. But there was one major problem: the culture there was basically corrupt. A lot of the company's finances were a total scam. Many of its debts and the losses did not appear in its financial statements, giving a false picture of Enron's health. In 2001, Enron filed for the biggest case of bankruptcy in the United States and 5,600 jobs were lost. They felt that they were invincible and simply didn't scrutinise carefully enough what was going wrong.

Are you able to relate what happened to Enron to an educational organisation that you have been involved with or know of?

Hot Tip: Culture is about the way they do things in the organisation; the norms, values and assumptions. You may have to do something if there is a mismatch between the culture that underpins your values and those of the organisation.

The final word on managing culture:

- Culture is about the way they do things in the organisation: the norms, values and assumptions.
- Ask yourself how you would define the existing culture in your organisation.
- Is your organisation driven by rules with little scope for flexibility or interaction between peers or is the emphasis on networks rather than individuals?
- Is decision-making shared by staff and students or are staff reluctant to share ideas, materials or solutions?
- If there is a mismatch between the culture that underpins your values and those of the organisation, do something about it.
- What culture does there needs to be for your leadership to flourish?
- How can you make the necessary changes to either the culture within the organisation or your leadership style?

14

PROJECT MANAGEMENT

Let's be clear here. If you are reading this section because you want to learn how to manage projects, then wise up; by virtue of the fact that you occupy a leadership position (or have demonstrated the capacity to be a leader), you have the skills required to manage projects. It's just that you haven't associated the skills set of a leader with those of a project manager.

At the start of the millennium, one of us helped the best part of 50 schools in the Gloucester, Worcester and West Midlands regions to write project bids to acquire funding for after-school clubs. It wasn't that staff in the schools lacked the ability to write the bids for these projects, it was either that they didn't have the time to spend researching and writing the bid or lacked confidence in their ability to put the bid together. In this chapter we cover the basics of good project management, how to research the need for the project and how to obtain funding for the project.

THE BASICS OF GOOD PROJECT MANAGEMENT

A project is a series of tasks or activities designed to bring about an agreed beneficial change or achieve some other identified objective within a fixed timeframe, using specified resources and to an acceptable level of quality. A useful way of looking at this is through the project triangle model (see Figure 14.1).

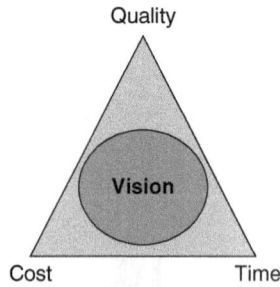

Figure 14.1   The project triangle model

The components in this model are:

Vision: What the project will achieve.

Time: When the project must be completed by.

Costs: What the budget for it is.

Quality: How it will be judged and by whom.

CASE STUDY

No compromise on quality: In November 1962, when the British and French governments agreed to develop and build the supersonic airliner, Concorde, they knew that there would have to be an exhaustive research and development programme before the aircraft could be certificated as meeting the aeronautical quality standards for passenger operation. Even those closest to the project did not at that time foresee the full-scale complexity and cost of this programme. The overall cost was nearly ten times the original estimates and time slippage nearly twice what was anticipated for the project. Until the 2000 Paris crash and its eventual scrapping, Concorde was considered to be the ultimate in luxury air travel and had the best safety record of any aircraft of its generation.

CASE STUDY

No compromise on time: Although the final bill for building the 2012 London Olympic stadium was well over twice the original estimate, there was absolutely no compromise on the deadline date. The consequences, in terms of PR and prestige, of the stadium not being ready on 27 July for the first event were too dire to contemplate.

CASE STUDY

No compromise on cost: Arguably one of the most expensive scandals in modern corporate history was the revelation that in 2015, Volkswagen cheated government emission testing. In an effort to work to budget and respond quickly to government environmental demands, Volkswagen engineers intentionally designed and installed a so called 'defeat device' (a piece of software rather than a physical device) into the engine's control computer. Prioritising cost and profit margin over quality and government regulations has shaken people's confidence in a once solid brand. The story is both an embarrassment for the company and a financial disaster for the shareholders. In addition to fines in excess of £12 billion, over £17 billion has been lost due to a drop in the company's stock price.

For most projects, there is unlikely to be any compromise on at least one of these components (possibly two). It is unlikely, however, that there will be no flexibility in all three components. Here is an exception to this rule.

CASE STUDY

No compromise full stop: Few major projects actually deliver in terms of their estimated costs, time and quality. One project that did was the Cornwall-based Eden project. Considered to be the largest greenhouse in the world, this was the brainchild of Tim Smit, an archaeologist and anthropology graduate who was born in Holland and educated at Durham University. In order to get public-sector funding for the project, Smit had to have a feasibility study that detailed how every penny would be spent. Anyone visiting this amazing site would be surprised to know that it only took 18 months from the first day of construction to opening its doors to visitors.

It was estimated that the unique and visionary warm temperate and humid tropics biomes that were the centrepiece of the Eden project would attract a maximum of 750,000 visitors a year and create 150 jobs. In its first year of full opening, the project saw 1.9 million visitors through its doors. In the second year the figure was 1.8 million and in the third year 1.4 million with 600 jobs created. Since then the visitor figure has levelled to around 1.2 million visitors a year. The costs of building the project were recovered within two years of opening. Smit's vision, inspirational leadership and refusal to compromise on quality have been the major contributors to the project's success.

Okay, so you're not planning to manage a project that involves flying the Atlantic in three hours or building a stadium or greenhouse that attracts millions of visitors or one that tries to con consumers (we certainly hope not!). You are, however, going to have to demonstrate to governors and sponsors that you have the necessary skills to take the project through from initial idea to fruition. Many of these skills are the same as those that any other manager should possess, in terms of managing human resources, schedules, budgets and quality control. Of course, if you have the luxury of a large team, you will have members of the team who will know more about some of these specifics than you do. Your job will be to motivate and get the best out of these people.

Reading the rest of this book will give you a good grounding in the skills outlined above. There are, however, two qualities that we feel deserve special mention and that, in some respect, will underpin everything that you do as a project manager:

> **Flexibility**: The structured approaches that we offer at key stages throughout this part of the book provide you with a logical framework to work to. They are not intended to be a millstone around your neck that means you always have to complete one task before moving on to the next. Never be afraid to revisit any of the tasks and modify them, especially if you have identified flawed assumptions made during any stages of the task.

> **Determination**: Great innovators such as Tim Smit and Steve Jobs had one thing in common: a determination to succeed despite critics who said it wasn't possible. If you are someone who is easily deterred by setbacks, then maybe project management isn't a job you should be doing. By all means listen to what people are saying and if they are making sense do something about it, but learn how to handle those people who just seem to be set on scuppering the project.

Assuming that you possess the above qualities the rest should be easy. Well, maybe not quite that easy. In an effort to make this section a meaningful and interesting read, we've tried to blend in some really great theoretical models with our own experiences of managing projects and some case studies of projects that were either great successes or disasters.

In the rest of this chapter, we cover three key areas of project management:

- Planning the project.
- Organising the project.
- Getting the funding to make it work.

Reading the rest of the chapter in conjunction with the chapters on Managing Budgets and Monitoring and Evaluation will give you the tools necessary to be an effective project manager.

RESEARCHING YOUR PROJECT

Taking time in the planning stage is very important as poor preparation usually means a poorly-performing project. In our experience, projects that do not start well because of poor planning rarely recover. Whether the project is building an extension to the school's toilet block or arranging a cultural exchange visit, take your time and make sure that you have established a solid foundation for the project and fully understand what the outcomes of the project are to be and what you must do to achieve these. Two critical questions to ask at this stage are:

- Who are the primary beneficiaries of the project?
- What can they expect from the project?

Don't even think about progressing with the project until you have answered these questions. Once you have answered the questions you need to think about:

- How will we do it?
- Who will do it and do we have the right skills to do it properly?
- When will we do it?
- What resources will we need?
- What will we need to monitor progress?
- How will we evaluate its success?

Organisations, their stakeholders and potential funders of the project will usually want to find out how the project is going to meet its aims and objectives and that it can deal with any problems that may occur. How a project intends to demonstrate this needs to be fully researched and clearly determined in the very early stages of planning. This process is often referred to as a *feasibility study*.

Feasibility studies represent the definition of a problem or opportunity to be studied, an analysis of the current mode of operation, a definition what's required to address the problem, an evaluation of alternatives and an agreed course of action.

There are basically five parts to any effective feasibility study:

Establish the project scope: This should be defined clearly and concisely. A rambling narrative serves no purpose here and can actually confuse project participants and potential funders.

Analyse the current situation: This is where you need to analyse what systems are already in place and what the strengths and weaknesses are of the current situation. Avoid the temptation to stop and correct any problems encountered in the current system at this time. Simply document your findings instead, otherwise you will spend more time unnecessarily in this stage.

Decide what resources are required to deal with the issue: These will vary considerably on the nature of the problem. Resources required for a change in the curriculum will be mostly time and brain power, whereas a modification to the school premises will involve external building contractors.

Determine the approach to be taken: This represents the recommended solution or course of action to satisfy the requirements. You need to make sure that you have considered as many alternative approaches as possible before arriving at the final one.

Review the feasibility of the venture: Once you begin to assemble all of the preceding elements into a feasibility study, a formal review should be conducted with all parties involved to substantiate the thoroughness and accuracy of the feasibility study, to assess the likely cost-effectiveness of the approach selected and to make a final decision on whether or not to progress with the venture.

It should be remembered that a feasibility study is more of a way of thinking as opposed to a bureaucratic process. The same process can be followed for staffing restructuring, timetable planning or major investments in new technology. In this respect, they represent a common-sense approach to planning and are just plain good business sense.

ORGANISING YOUR PROJECT

In the research phase of your plan, you should have a clear picture of why the project is necessary. Now begins the task of implementing the plan. This should involve having a schedule for who will do what, where, how and when, and a contingency plan for what to do if something goes wrong.

Gerry Johnson and Kevin Scholes developed a seven-stage approach that they suggested would produce a comprehensive and structured schedule for developing a project. The key point underpinning each stage is:

Mission: Have a vision of what the project will achieve and a determination to get there.

Goals: Identify what goals must be achieved in order to realise the vision.

Objectives: Break down the goals into specific, measurable, acceptable, realistic and time-bound (SMART) objectives.

Strategy: Determine what actions are necessary to achieve the objectives.

Actions: Execute the strategy.

Control: Set up a process for evaluating progress.

Rewards: Celebrate success.

Whether you are looking to make minor changes to the school timetable or planning a major refurbishment of the school, even in the most modest of projects there are steps that you can take to ensure success:

- Share your vision for the project with people who are likely to have a stake in the project. Express the vision in terms of what benefits stakeholders will accrue from the project.

- Set down the goals that the project needs to achieve in order to realise this vision.
- Break down the goals into tasks that are specific, measurable, acceptable, realistic, timebound.
- Organise the project team into subgroups or individuals who will be expected to complete each task.
- Monitor performance and address any shortfalls in actual against planned performance.
- Don't wait until you have achieved the vision before opening the champagne; celebrate small successes en route and recognise each individual's contribution.

CASE STUDY

Pam's experience of project development and management was that purposeful planning was frequently undermined during the action stage and that inadequate control strategies failed to adequately evaluate the successes and shortfalls. She contributed this in part to the fact that more often than not those who were concerned with the implementation and running of the project were also responsible for monitoring and evaluation. Therefore, at the outset of a project to improve assessment of learning Pam identified a separate quality control team whose members did not have a key role to play in the planning, implementation and running of the project.

In identifying separate roles for the implementers and evaluators she enabled each to focus more successfully on their roles. Pam took great care to personally monitor and evaluate the success of the project, and in particular the performance of the quality control team. There were enough positives to subsequently build upon and use as the model for future projects in the organisation.

Although he died nearly a hundred years before Pam set to work on her project, Henry Gantt, an American Engineer, may have helped her. Gantt designed a method of charting progress towards an end product. A very simplified version of a Gantt chart that depicts four key activities in the project life cycle to be conducted over a six month period would look something like that shown in Figure 14.2.

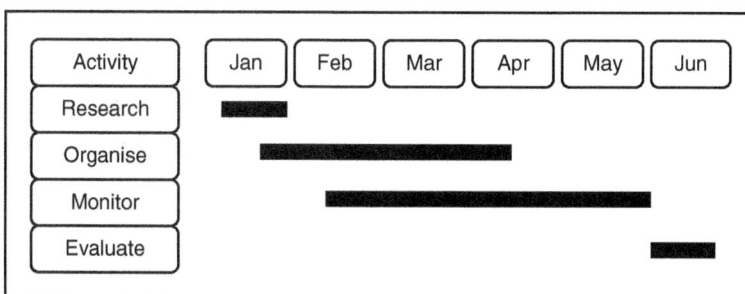

Figure 14.2 The Gantt model

Notice how activities such as research, organise and monitor overlap. The chart helps you to think about what time you need to introduce and complete various activities by. Most Gantt charts start from day one through to the project completion date. An alternative approach which we quite like is to start with the end product and keep working backwards until you get to the beginning of the implementation stage.

There's a classic scene in Lewis Carroll's *Alice in Wonderland* where Alice asks the Cheshire cat 'Which way to go from here?'. The Cat asks, 'That depends a good deal on where you want to get to.' Alice replies, 'I don't much care where.' To which the Cat answers, 'Then it doesn't matter which way you go.' **Matthew Batchelor** (2010) refers to this as *the backward pass*. He suggests looking at the end result and asking yourself 'What do I need to do immediately before I can achieve this?', then keep asking yourself the same question until you get to the starting point of the project.

There are many variations of Gantt charts. See www.gantt.com or www.ganttchart.com for examples of these. They are excellent tools but not infallible, and you must guard against things that will scupper your plans.

Robert Burns once wrote that 'The best-laid schemes o' mice an' men gang aft agley, an' lea'e us nought but grief an' pain, for promis'd joy!' Of course, despite all of your meticulous planning and scheduling, as Burns warns you, something could go wrong. You can curse (not too loudly though) when this happens or you can try and guard against it happening by trying to anticipate what could go wrong and having a strategy in place for preventing this.

Let's be realistic here. You can worry that much about bad things happening that you talk yourself out of ever starting the project (we know many head teachers who fell at the first hurdle when managing a project and many who didn't even try and get over it). Also some events that will hinder the project will be so out of your control that despite all your efforts to prevent or minimise the risks associated with them, they will happen anyway. You will need an approach therefore that will grade the risks according to their likelihood and their severity.

A useful way of doing this is make a list of all possible risks associated with the project. Grade each risk according to its severity (the damage that it can cause the project it if materialises) on a scale of 1 (none at all) to 10 (crippling). Then grade each risk according to its likelihood (the dangers of it occurring), again on a scale of 1 (none at all) to 10 (certain). Then multiply the two factors together.

All risks that have a residual score of over 80 *must* be addressed urgently, and you will need to know in no uncertain terms what you are going to do if they become a reality. Better still, take action to minimise the possibility of them occurring, as the time doing this may be less than the time having to take action if they do occur. Of course taking action to prevent them happening in the first place is the ideal but may be costly in terms of time and money. You will have to make a judgement call on this.

All risks that have a residual score of 60–79 *should* be addressed urgently if the higher-rated risks have been dealt with and they can be tackled without utilising valuable resources.

All risks that have a residual score of 40–59 *could* be addressed if the other higher-rated risks have been dealt with and they can be tackled without too much effort.

Don't think that you can forget about the risks that have a residual score of 20–39 as they can have a negative effect on the project. Consider taking action to reduce the likelihood of the risk happening, but again you need to make a judgement call and ask whether the costs of dealing with these risks outweigh the risk itself.

Of course you can forget about the risks that have a residual score of less than 20. Well, maybe not altogether. They may not happen, and if they do, may not a have disastrous effect on the project. Perhaps best to take a gamble and just accept them if they do happen or deal with them if you have some spare time.

Whatever you decide in terms of managing risks to the project, sponsors will want to see that you have a contingency plan to use if the risk does become a reality. We'd be very rich if we had a pound for every potential sponsor who has said 'but what if?'. Demonstrating that you have a countermeasure (or better still countermeasures) for dealing with the 'what ifs?' will stand you in good stead with sponsors.

> **Hot Tip:** Deal with all high likelihood/high severity risks immediately. Consider what risks can be deferred or delegated. Only deal with low likelihood/low severity risks if you have nothing better to do.

GETTING THE FUNDING FOR YOUR PROJECT

Reading Chapter 10 will give you some idea of estimating the cost of delivering the project. The next step is to secure the funding to make it happen. If anyone ever claims to have a method for guaranteeing they can obtain funding for projects, then they are either very clever or very stupid. There is no blueprint that will guarantee success in any bid. One of us wrote two very similar lottery bids for the same project idea in two very similar schools in the same geographical area – only to find out that one was successful and one failed. It just goes to show there are many frustrations that accompany bid writing.

Despite these setbacks, we have both had many bids that were successful and have learned over the years that there are some steps that you can take which might significantly reduce the odds on the bid not being successful. These make up what we refer to as the *cars, boats and shotgun weddings* model.

STEP 1: DECIDE WHAT YOUR STRATEGY FOR SEEKING FUNDS IS

Are you looking for funds to support existing work within the organisation? Or are you looking to shape existing work to match a funding opportunity? There are no real problems with either approach. Some might say the former is more principled, some might say the latter is more for survival. Where it does become problematic is when you look to completely sacrifice or radically change what you were set up to achieve for the sake of obtaining funding.

If an organisation manufactures cars and there is money available to make boats, what should they do? Expertise in making vehicles that run on roads and rely on traction power doesn't automatically mean the organisation can easily adapt to making vehicles that run on water and rely on wind power. They may have skills within the organisation that can be utilised in order to make boats but the risk to the organisation's reputation should the venture fail may mean future funding for making cars might be withheld.

Of course you can compromise and make an amphibious vehicle that can travel at good speeds on both land and sea. James Bond, played by Sir Roger Moore, famously drove an amphibious Lotus Esprit from the land into the sea during the 1977 film *The Spy Who Loved Me*. You no longer need to be a spy like James Bond to get your hands on an amphibious car. A California-based company, WaterCar, has designed the world's fastest Jeep-style vehicle that can be driven straight from the land into the water and goes from a car to a boat in just 15 seconds. It can reach water speeds of up to 45 mph – almost as fast as an average speedboat.

We use this analogy to demonstrate that projects can diversify successfully, as a prerequisite for either survival or growth, providing they don't stray too far from their basic mission. We're not sure how much we agree with Tom Peter's adage of 'sticking to the knitting' (only do what you are good at doing), but we do think that straying too far from what you have a reputation for being good at can have a negative effect on the organisation. Are you old enough to remember Clive Sinclair's disastrous attempts to move from making computers to cars?

STEP 2: KEEP A WATCHFUL EYE ON FUNDING OPPORTUNITIES

Obtaining funding for a commercial product may be slightly different from doing so for an educational or social venture. Financial institutions are more likely to fund something that is tangible and can be sold, whereas local and central government departments and lottery funders are more interested in projects that benefit local communities. Banks will want to see a business plan that shows a projected financial return on their investment. Local and central government are more interested in the social return on their investment.

STEP 3: CARRY OUT THE NECESSARY RESEARCH

Funding applications can be very brief or depressingly extensive. UK Lottery bids for quite large amounts are relatively brief (because they want to encourage community groups to apply), whereas Local Authority bids, even for small amounts, can run into dozens of pages (because they are accountable for all spend to committees). Read through the bid carefully and make sure that you can support your bid with properly researched evidence.

STEP 4: GET HELP IN PUTTING THE BID TOGETHER

This doesn't mean employing a consultant or bid-writer (unless you don't have that expertise in your organisation), but it may mean talking to people who may have specialist knowledge or understanding that they can contribute. Most funding bodies are now loathe to approve funding for single-applicant organisations and like to see partnership elements in the bid. If you adopt this approach, make sure that the partners understand what commitments they are making and what benefits they will get from being a partner. You may have to enter into some partnerships against your will. This is where you have to make a value judgement as to whether it's worthwhile entering into the arrangement.

STEP 5: WRITE THE BID IN THE APPROPRIATE MANNER AND STYLE

Good bid writers learn how to write the bid in a clear, concise manner. Funding assessors will not want to read through pages and pages of flowery script. They will also not just want to see you regurgitating what's in their commissioning letter. They will want to see that some effort has gone into the research and writing of the bid and that you can demonstrate your ability to deliver what they want. Show the bid to others in your organisation – if they can't understand what the bid is about, what chance will funders have when it comes to them assessing the bid?

STEP 6: GET IT RIGHT FIRST TIME

Very often, because of the competitive nature of the bidding process, and especially where electronic bidding is concerned, you won't get an opportunity to revise any aspect of the bid once it has been submitted. Look out for any added value aspects in your idea. Although there may be a main theme to your bid, there may be additional factors that attract the attention of the funders. Don't, however, go overboard with this and lose sight of what the funds are intended to achieve.

A useful tip here is to find out if the funders use a grid for assessing the bid. If they do, then make sure that you get hold of it and write your bid so as to address each point in the grid. For example, if a large chunk of the scoring in the assessment grid relates to innovation or partnership working, put a massive amount of time and effort into explaining how innovative your project is going to be or how your partnership working is going to function.

Without becoming obsessive about it read, reread and reread once more to check you have got everything right. Two gaffs that one of us committed that we're not too proud to share with you were writing a proposal for funding a talking newsletter for the deaf and one for a centre for depraved kids. Luckily, the prospective funders recognised that we'd had junior moments in both instances, and the bids were successful with many blind people and deprived children benefitting.

STEP 7: PERSEVERE WITH BIDDING EVEN IF YOU ARE EXPERIENCING FAILURE

Most funding organisations (including some financial institutions) will give you feedback as to why your bid was unsuccessful. If the funds are important, keep a look out for the next bidding opportunity and address the points raised in the feedback. Of course this is no guarantee of success – if they don't want to give you the money, they will simply find other reasons to fail your application. We guess one of you will back down eventually and they will give you the money or you'll take your bid elsewhere.

You may think that we're being cynical here. No funding body will ever admit that they are nothing but totally objective when it comes to assessing bids and moves, especially by funders for voluntary and community projects. In becoming more transparent in the bidding process through allowing projects access to scoring grids and electronic initial screening of bids, they have taken some of the subjectivity out of the process. There is, however, always a human element involved in assessing bids and, where this exists, scope for subjectivity. We're afraid that unless you have intimate knowledge of those involved in the assessment it's simply a case of some you win, some you lose.

STEP 8: FINALLY, ONCE THE BID HAS GONE OFF, DON'T WALK ACROSS THE PATH OF ANY BLACK CATS OR UNDER LADDERS

Despite efforts on the part of funding bodies to make the assessment as fair as possible, there is still a lot of luck attached to this process. On the right day at the right moment, a bid may be seen in a better light than on another day. You can't legislate for this and although most funders will claim that they have a process and marking system that are fair and entirely objective, our experiences of writing project bids tell us that luck does play a big part. The important thing is to be honest with yourself. You may be competing with others for a share of the money. If you have given it your best shot but lose out to a better bid, then so be it. The only time for self-recrimination is if you haven't given it your best!

Use the SMARTER checklist in Figure 14.3 to review a bid that you have put together.

☐ **S**pecific: Have you made it clear what the project is about? Is there an early statement of intent?

☐ **M**easurable: Have you made it clear how many people will benefit from the project?

☐ **A**mbitious: Are you likely to impress with your project's aims and objectives? But

☐ **R**ealistic: Are you being realistic about what you can actually achieve with the project?

☐ **T**imescales: Have you set out tasks or milestones for what you want to achieve?

☐ **E**nthusiastic: Have you created the impression of being a project team that will deliver and be able to overcome minor setbacks?

☐ **R**esearch Evidence: Have you demonstrated that the project has been well-researched?

Figure 14.3 The SMARTER planning tool

Hot Tip: If you have a project bid ready to submit to a sponsor, see how many of the SMARTER boxes you could tick with confidence.

A final word on project management:

- Share your vision for the project with people who are likely to have a stake in the project.
- Express the vision in terms of what benefits stakeholders will accrue from the project.
- Set down the goals that the project needs to achieve in order to realise this vision.
- Break down the goals into tasks that are specific, measurable, acceptable, realistic, timebound.
- Organise the project team into subgroups or individuals who will be expected to complete each task.
- Monitor performance and address any shortfalls in actual against planned performance.
- Don't wait until you have achieved the vision before opening the champagne; celebrate small successes en route and recognise each individual's contribution.
- Determine what your strategy for seeking funds is.
- Understand what elements go into effective bidding.
- Know the importance of carrying out the necessary research.
- Appreciate the need to get help in putting the bid together.
- Write the bid in the appropriate manner and style.
- Persevere with bidding even if you are experiencing failure.
- Use the SMARTER checklist to review a bid that you have put together.
- Accept the need to evaluate the project using the funder's criteria, not based on your own organisational objectives.
- Have a plan for dealing with risks.
- Have a process for evaluating the impact of your project.

15
MONITORING AND EVALUATION

Monitoring and evaluation are complementary management tools. There are, however, differences in that monitoring is concerned with the periodical collection of data and information collection for tracking progress whereas evaluation focuses on the eventual outcomes and impact that the organisation has achieved. Let's look at this in more detail.

MONITORING

There are generally four key aspects of performance that needs to be monitored. These are:

Inputs: These include staff time as well as equipment and materials.

Outputs: These are the organisation's performance results.

Outcomes: These are the effects that the results have on learners and the wider community.

Impact: This covers the longer-term or broader changes occurring as a result of the outcomes.

Think about this in terms of a grapevine. *Inputs* are the cost and time related to the planting and nurturing of the vine. *Outputs* are the numbers of grapes produced. An *outcome is* the quality of the wine produced. *Impact* is the reputation of the wine makers that will be enhanced by a quality wine.

If we extend the wine analogy, we can see that it is relatively easy to keep a check on inputs. This will include the costs associated with the seedlings, fertilisers, canes, netting, bottles and so on plus the cost of the staff time involved in all aspects of the process (buying, planting, reaping, meshing, bottling, marketing, delivery, management etc.). Outputs are even easier: here this will simply be a count of the number of grapes produced. Outcomes are more difficult: they require a judgement about the quality of the wine produced. These judgements can be *objective*, in that they are measured against criteria set down by the wine industry, or *subjective*, based what the consumer likes or dislikes.

Measuring impact is easily the most difficult aspect of the whole process. In the analogy, it might include delighted or disgruntled consumers of the product, an enhanced or ruined reputation within the wine industry and jobs created or lost.

Hot Tip: Performance monitoring is essential but it's only one part of the planning process. Focusing all of your energies on chasing performance indicators may be counter-productive.

EVALUATION

Evaluation is a systematic appraisal of the organisation's merit, worth and significance. It can have either an internal or external focus: Internal in that it is something that everyone in the organisation should be doing within their area of responsibility as a self-improvement tool, and external to provide evidence of the organisation's impact. It is often based on criteria governed by a set of internal or external standards. It can assist an organisation to ascertain the degree of achievement in regard to its educational aims and objectives. It gives meaning to the predicted or actual outputs or performance results.

The word 'evaluation' has various connotations for different people. This raises issues related to the process that include:

- Why do we need to evaluate the organisation?
- What type of evaluation should be conducted?
- Who should be conducting the evaluation?
- How can the evaluation be integrated into how the organisation performs?

This is where an organisation uses the monitoring information and other information it collects to make an informed judgement about how effectively the organisation is performing (formative evaluation) or has performed (summative evaluation). If the monitoring has been done and recorded in a systematic and structured manner, the organisation should have:

- A detailed account of all inputs, outputs and outcomes.
- A profile of all information on learners and other beneficiaries.
- Statistical information on recruitment and retention.
- A record of any complaints and compliments from stakeholders.

An issue to bear in mind here is that interested bodies such as local authorities some-times have a habit of asking for additional information when the operational year is well underway. Second-guessing what information may be required is difficult, so, from the outset, sit down with those concerned bodies and agree a list of what items they want you to monitor and what format they want the evaluation report in. If you do this, then requests for additional information may be considered unreasonable. You may take a stand on this but in my experience knowing when to back down on an issue with the authorities is one of the key attributes of good leadership.

The real issue is how to effectively garner information in order to make telling evaluations. You therefore need to think clearly about where the focus of the evalua-tion will be and who and where you want to obtain information from. Make sure that you set aside enough time and resources to gather this information. This might involve a combination of *quantitative* analysis (outputs) and *qualitative* analysis (outcomes). You may want to do this in house. This can sometimes be done quickly, providing you have suitably trained staff to do it, and is relatively inexpensive, but you may be accused of being biased in your findings. You may want to commission external evaluators, which may take time to organise and possibly expensive but can deflect claims of bias.

> **Hot Tip**: The quality of evaluation depends upon the expertise of the evaluators.

Using the evaluation findings effectively will:

- Justify its existence and expenditure to the authorities, funders, stakeholders and the general public
- Make use of the findings to feed back into, and guide, the management of the organisation and possibly influence a change in policy or practice.

Justification and learning are the two critical aspects of evaluation. A useful model to use here is **Chris Argyris** and **Donald Schön**'s (2002) *triple loop learning*. In this model, Argyris and Schön claim that organisational learning can be characterised in terms of a three-level evolutionary model consisting of single, double and triple-loop learning. This can be represented as shown in Figure 15.1.

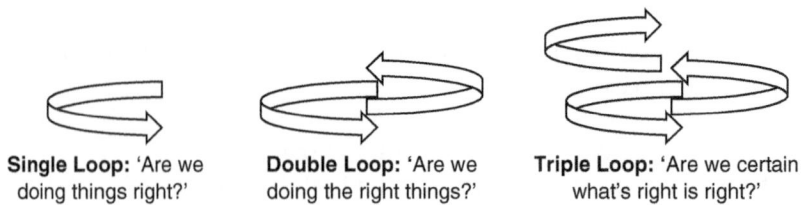

Single Loop: 'Are we doing things right?'   **Double Loop:** 'Are we doing the right things?'   **Triple Loop:** 'Are we certain what's right is right?'

Figure 15.1   The triple loop model

Each of these loops can be summarised as follows:

- **Single-loop** learning is the basic level of measuring the efficiency of the organisation and the activities being undertaken, and is connected to error detection and correction. It asks the question, 'Are we doing things right in our organisation?'
- **Double-loop** learning is more geared towards measuring the effectiveness of the organisation, and focuses on error prevention throughout the organisation, not just at the point of delivery. It asks the question, 'Are we doing the right things in our organisation?'
- **Triple-loop** learning represents the highest form of self-examination and involves constantly questioning the organisation. It asks the question, 'How can we be sure what we consider to be right with our organisation is right?'

CASE STUDY

Monitoring is an essential process in gathering information about a school, project or initiative. The time invested in monitoring is only rewarded if it is used to evaluate effectiveness. This is not always the case when leaders do not have sufficient training and time.

Failure to evaluate effectively is not only limited to schools. In July 2010 the coalition government announced that, starting in April 2011, schools would receive a new pupil premium to raise achievement among disadvantaged children. Michael Gove, the then secretary of state for education, described schools as 'engines of social mobility', suggesting that narrowing the gaps in achievement between pupils from disadvantaged backgrounds and other pupils was a priority. Schools were charged with using this money to narrow the attainment gap in performance between these pupils and others. This is monitored in Ofsted inspections and the yearly Ofsted statistical releases.

However, four years later there has only been a slight reduction in the attainment gaps between disadvantaged and other pupils by the time they leave primary school. Disadvantaged pupils are still over two terms behind other pupils, the gap having been reduced by just over two weeks. Effective evaluation of the outcomes of the pupil premium initiative would surely have raised questions regarding the usefulness of this initiative.

While it's not just the quality of your teaching and learning that dictates whether your organisation is outstanding, let's be honest and say this is at the heart of what you do and if you haven't got this right you may as well pack up. Too often the emphasis is built on the old quality control processes of *inspection–detection–rectification–retribution*: let's look at what we're doing in our classrooms, let's detect errors, let's put them right and let's find out who's to blame. If this is what your organisation is doing, you have stalled in single-loop learning.

So, how do you get out of single-loop? Here are some things to think about:

■ Do not get engrossed in the blame culture. Okay! So people make mistakes. The essence of d-loop learning is to learn from these mistakes. All right, if the same people in your organisation keep making the same mistakes you will have to do something about them (see the chapter on Human Resource Management).

■ So, well done! By an enthusiastic application of double-loop learning you have assured the quality of your teaching and learning. Let's sit back and wait for the praise to roll in. Actually no! Other organisations competing with you for learners have also read Argyris and Schön and have done the same. Someone with an underperforming college that was losing learners to another college once asked me, 'What can we do to catch up with them?' I told them, 'I wasn't aware they were waiting for you' (see the chapter on Managing Quality).

■ Don't think that, like Bruce Banner transforming into the Hulk, transformation has to be that dramatic. It may be about addressing a few small things like changing the colour on your organisation's promotional literature or how you deal with people on the phone (see the chapter on Managing Change).

■ Don't sit back and wait for things to happen. If this is the culture in your organisation, then do something about it and get out there and look for areas for improvement. It's important for you to learn from mistakes but it's also important to catch people out doing something good and see what you can learn from this (see the chapter on Culture).

> **Hot Tip:** Remember you may be evaluating the organisation against the criteria set by the authorities, not necessarily by your own organisational objectives.

Monitoring and evaluating are all about learning; learning what works and what doesn't work in a systematic way. Bypass either of these stages, or go through them in a half-hearted manner, and you may as well have not started in the first place. Don't fall into the trap of paralysis by analysis but do have some form of capturing and analysing the data from your monitoring and evaluation and use this to inform your planning.

The most important thing to remember is that you don't have all the answers, and to make sure that you involve others (stakeholders, staff, learners and other beneficiaries) in the planning process, and don't be afraid if some blue-sky thinking occurs.

After all, who would have thought that putting dead leaves in your mouth and setting them alight would become a multi-billion pound industry?

A final word on monitoring and evaluation:

- Don't rush through the processes of monitoring and evaluation; each of them will have a massive impact on the success of the organisation.
- Remember you may be evaluating the organisation against the criteria set by the authorities, not necessarily by your own organisational objectives.
- Have a process for evaluating the impact of your organisation.
- The quality of evaluation depends upon the expertise of the evaluators.
- Do not get engrossed in the blame culture.
- Don't get complacent by early successes.
- Accept that transformation may be about addressing a few small things.
- Don't sit back and wait for things to happen.
- Look to catch people out doing something good and see what you can learn from this.

16

MANAGING
COMMUNICATION

Leadership is about people. There are technical things that you can learn that, to be honest, are skills that anyone has the capacity to learn. Effective leadership, however, is about getting people to move in a certain direction and to get things done. To do this you need to be a good communicator. These are skills that can also be learned but may require a greater level of application than some of the more technical skills.

To prove the importance of communication, one of us used to tell the story of how the message relayed along the line from the trenches to the command post to 'Send reinforcements, we're going to advance' was interpreted as 'Send three and four pence we're going to dance'. Unfortunately after forty years of currency decimalisation this no longer makes sense. Instead, he now uses the following: *The dissemination of information for one's maternal predecessor may be prejudiced towards the avoidance of avian derived ovum, utilising vacuum induction.*

If you are already a great communicator and can understand this, and believe it to be true, then you may as well skip this section. If not, we'll translate it for you in the final paragraph – but you must promise us that you'll read the rest of the section.

Harold Lasswell (1979) introduced an important model of five phases of communication in the late 1940s. This was later referred to as the 'five Ws', elements of which survive in more developed modern models. Lasswell's model covers the following:

- **Who**?: the sender
- says **what**?: the message
- through **which** Channel?: through what channel or medium

- to **whom**?: the receiver
- with **what** effect in mind?: the desired effect.

Figure 16.1 is a basic representation of Lasswell's model to which we have added a feedback loop from the *receiver* to the *sender*. This is an important phase in the process to ensure that the message has been interpreted as the sender intended.

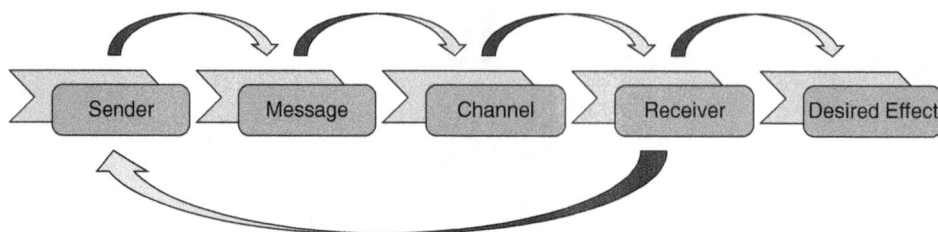

Figure 16.1 The communication model

Addressing the 'five Ws' is an essential element of all communication; getting this right is the first step in the process and is dependent upon what is required to be communicated at the time.

Who should control the communications process? This should be the most appropriate person depending on the individuals, the subject and the desired outcome. Things that have a direct impact on staff should always come from the person in charge.

What should they be told? Always give clear messages, related to the subject or problem.

How should the message be conveyed? Choose the most effective medium to get your message across; this could be in meetings, seminars, press releases and so on. Make time to communicate properly; do not do it in the corridor, in the toilet or the car park as this leads to gabbled and garbled messages and can contribute to the 'grapevine'.

Who should be told? Everyone who needs to be told about something should be told. It is advisable to relate the communication to all as soon as possible. Openness is the key to making everyone feel involved (although there will always be some things which are not disseminated as widely as others). Where appropriate, communicate widely so that individuals are given the opportunity to influence the process and local ownership is gained. Barriers can also be identified and overcome.

How can you be sure that the message has been understood? In complex situations it is advisable to create a shared meaning and understanding. This can be done by checking back with the recipients through an iterative process that lets them ask questions, seeking clarification of what they have understood, and being clear that words, behaviours and symbols are not misunderstood or misinterpreted.

The time to communicate with relevant people should be carefully considered. It might be within a set staff meeting or a one-off arrangement. If the communication covers a wide range of people, where possible it is desirable that discussions take place at the same time to avoid confusion, the spreading of rumours or misunderstandings. If internal and external stakeholders are involved, we suggest that in most instances internal staff should be communicated with prior to external stakeholders; this is to prevent staff hearing from other sources, including the media.

Eric Berne (2010) suggested that the way we regard ourselves and those we interact with influences our attitudes and emotional states and hence the way we communicate with them. He represented this theory in a 2x2 matrix with one axis depicting the level of value of others (I'm okay with you) and the other one its own self-value (I'm okay with me). Not surprisingly this is sometimes called the 'OK Corral' model (see Figure 16.2).

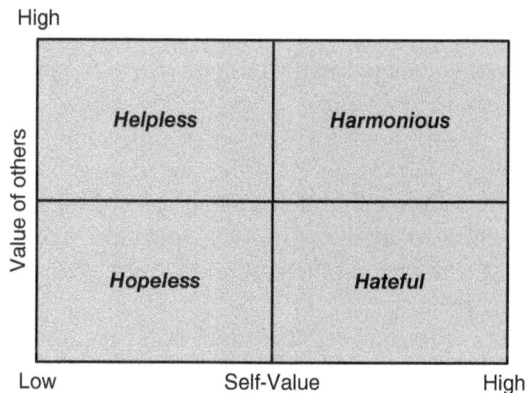

Figure 16.2   The 'OK Corral' model

The characteristics of the four quadrants are:

I'm not okay with me – I'm not okay with you: This is the *hopeless*, or get nowhere situation, characterised by frustration and accusations of blame by both parties.

I'm okay with me – I'm not okay with you: This is the *hateful*, or get rid of situation, characterised by anger and trying to get one up on the other person.

I'm not okay with me – I'm okay with you: This is the *helpless*, or get away from situation, characterised by fear and allowing the other person to get one up on you.

I'm okay with me – I'm okay with you: This is the *harmonious*, or get on with situation, characterised by constructive and cooperative relationships.

Many have used Berne's theory to learn how to challenge their old belief systems about why they are 'not okay' and replace them with more constructive thoughts about how they feel about themselves and others.

Berne's model is brilliant, not just because of its simplicity but also because of its inspirational qualities. You cannot ignore the message, regardless of what interactions you have in your leadership role. Having low self-value and not valuing the other person is quite simply a hopeless situation. Having good self-value and valuing the other person on the other hand is a happy, harmonious one.

Recognising where you are on the model is one thing, doing something about is where the hard bit comes in. It's easy to change your outlook towards the other person if you can get beyond the negativity that may be clouding your judgement. One of us was leading on an education programme for offenders who had committed the most serious of crimes; one of the tutors was adamant that they were there to educate the offenders, not to judge them. She took the view that if they wanted to learn, she would do her utmost to help them achieve. This indicated not just the value of the other person but also a high sense of self-value; she was doing something she believed in.

The difficult bit is raising your own sense of self-value. We don't know where you stand on the nature–nurture debate. The question is 'Are people born with a lack of self-belief or is it hammered into them?' There's a lot said about self-fulfilling prophecies – keep telling someone they're stupid and guess what? Keep telling yourself you're stupid and the implications are even clearer. Positive self-talk is something you should practise.

Did we refer to this model as the 'OK Corral'? Let's take another trip to the cinema and the 1957 classic western film *Gunfight at the O.K. Corral*:

Wyatt Earp (played by Burt Lancaster) is a legendary lawman who joins his brothers to help them in a feud with the Clantons, a gang of cattle thieves led by Ike Clanton (played by Lyle Bettger). The Earps are joined in the inevitable shoot out by Doc Holliday (played by Kirk Douglas), a terminally ill drunk and gambler. In this film we see thugs, drunks, villains, murderers (and they were just the good guys) fighting it out.

The film is a classic case of people on both sides with low senses of value of themselves and others interacting with people of the same conviction. The outcome was that a few got killed and some badly injured. I'll leave it you to work out what lessons can be learned from this.

Eric Berne also suggested that the state of mind we are in when we communicate with people will influence how the other person receives, interprets or acts on the communication. He proposed five states of mind, or *ego states*, that people use when communicating.

These can be represented as the:

Critical parent state: This is where the leader is overbearing towards others and tells them what to do because they believe their way is the correct one.

Nurturing parent state: This is where the leader expresses concern for others and offers advice and support.

Free child state: This is where the leader is not afraid to share their feelings with others.

Adaptive child state: This is where the leader feels inhibited in expressing themself in front of others.

Adult state: This is where the leader acts by expressing themself in a calm and rational manner.

Berne stresses that the terms *parent, child* and *adult* have nothing to do with age or relationships but act as metaphors to describe the state of mind people adopt. He also argues that, although behaving in the *adult* state is generally the most effective practitioner approach, there may be times when being in the *parent* or even the *child* state might get results.

CASE STUDY

Naomi was near the end of what had been a very intense discussion with a member of staff who had initially been in a highly distressed and aggressive state. As the discussion went on it became apparent that the member of staff had been attempting to deal with some very difficult personal issues to which Naomi was naturally sympathetic and had tried to reach out to her by sharing a past problem of her own, which in the retelling had caused Naomi at one moment to 'well-up' slightly. The meeting then appeared to end convivially, only for Naomi to learn later that the member of staff had not only shared Naomi's anecdote about her past in the staffroom, but accused her of being over-emotional and showing signs of weakness.

> **Hot Tip**: Ask yourself: Am I sure that I am in the right frame of mind when I communicate with the person I am managing? Do I appreciate what frame of mind they are in? Have I chosen the right ego state for the communication that will achieve a long-term satisfactory outcome?

Even if you have a high sense of self-value and value for others and are in the right frame of mind, accept that it might not work perfectly for everyone in every given situation and that occasionally you might end up with egg on your face. Oh, by the way, on the subject of eggs, the answer to the question posed in the introduction is, *'Don't teach your granny to suck eggs'*.

The final word on communication:

■ Ask who should control the communications process.
■ Decide what they should be told.
■ Determine how the message should be conveyed.
■ Who should be told?
■ Question if you can be sure that the message has been understood.
■ Ask yourself 'Am I sure that I am in the right frame of mind when I communicate with the person I am managing?'
■ Ask yourself 'Do I appreciate what frame of mind they are in?'
■ Decide if you have chosen the right ego state for the communication that will achieve a long-term satisfactory outcome.

17

MANAGING TIME

Okay, we've all been there. We are working on a new programme and the pressure's on. The deadline, like an express train, is hurtling towards us. We've only got half the necessary tasks completed. Suppliers aren't doing what they said they'd do and senior management are turning the screws. Like a rabbit staring into the headlights, we're paralysed by fear (phew, we're starting to sweat ourselves). Nobody in the team seems to share our concern about the programme's inactivity or failure to meet deadlines. What do we do? We lie back and think of America – well two Americans actually. Between them, Eisenhower and Stephen Covey have given us a simple yet effective way of managing time efficiently and effectively.

The approach is based on a quote from former American president Dwight Eisenhower: 'What is important is seldom urgent and what is urgent is seldom important'. **Stephen Covey** (2004) popularised the principle as forming one of the seven habits of highly effective people. The principle is generally represented as a 2×2 matrix with low to high importance on one axis and low to high urgency on the other.

The characteristics of each of the quadrants in the matrix are:

> **High Importance – High Urgency (HIHU)**: These are tasks that are critical to the project and have to be done immediately.
>
> **High Importance – Low Urgency (HILU)**: These are tasks that will have an impact on the project but don't have to be done immediately.

Low Importance – High Urgency (LIHU): These are tasks that need to be done immediately but can be delegated.

Low Importance – Low Urgency (LILU): These are minor distractions and should be avoided.

Covey argues that by using the matrix to prioritise you can deal with the urgent tasks whilst at the same time working towards achieving your long-term project goals. Do this by:

- Compiling a list of all of the things that you need to do (even the unimportant things). Write these on a separate card.
- Dividing your desk into four quarters (representing the quadrants in the matrix).
- Placing each card in the respective quarters denoting HIHU – HILU – LIHU – LILU (does this sound like an audition for a yodelling choir?).
- Taking out those cards in the LILU quarter of the desk and shredding them! Hang on – before doing that, just check to see if any of them have the potential to become LIHUs. If they do, then don't shred them just yet.
- Now work on the HIHU quarter. Take each activity card in turn, put them in order of priority and take the necessary action to deal with the activity. With some activities, a little bit of action might relegate them to the HILU or LIHU quarters. Don't stop until you have cleared all of the activities in that quarter.
- This is where you make a choice of dealing with the HILU or LIHU activities. I suggest that if time is incredibly tight you go for LIHU first. If you have more time to play around with go for HILU. Don't stop until you have cleared all of the activities in those quarters.
- Now go back to the LILU quarter and deal with all of the activities left, shredding the ones that are nothing more than distractions.

Wasn't that fun? Please don't tell us that you didn't have the time to do it!

Having a strategy for prioritising tasks is important. We now deal with the vexing question of how you can deal with interruptions that prevent you from completing the tasks. Interruptions can be a major barrier to managing your time effectively. In order to have a strategy for dealing with them you are going to have to devote a little bit of your valuable time. Yes, we know that you have more pressing things to do – trust us, it will benefit you in the long run.

- Start by keeping a daily log of interruptions that occur. Do this over the course of a week. Record what the interruption was, who interrupted you, the degree of importance attached to the interruption (a simple high–medium–low or rating from 1–10 will suffice) and how long the whole interaction lasted.
- Analyse whether the interruption was valid. Ask whether it needed to be dealt with immediately or could have been delayed or avoided.
- Accept that some interruptions are necessary and require urgent action. You can deal with unnecessary interruptions by saying 'I can't discuss this now'. If you

do this, make sure you allocate space at a more convenient time when you can discuss it.

- Appreciate that although the issue may be of low importance/urgency to you, it may not be this way for the person interrupting you. Giving them the brush-off may not do much for your reputation as a caring manager.
- Learn to say 'No'. Doing this in a polite and courteous manner followed by a short explanation is the assertive way of dealing with an interruption that prevents you from doing more important/urgent things.

An important part of the leadership role is to be available to people, to deal with important issues and to make your staff as effective as possible. Giving unlimited access to your time will prevent you from doing this. Imposing barriers to accessibility that are too high, however, will have the same effect.

Okay, so we all know that we could be managing our time more effectively. The results of this are simple: we become more productive in our work and our stress levels drop. Time is a commodity, however, and over-using it can sometimes have dire consequences. Let's take yet another trip to the cinema and the 1986 film *Clockwise* to see how this can happen:

In the film, Brian Stimpson, played by John Cleese, is an obsessively punctual head-master of a large secondary school in England. The opening scenes see him setting himself, his staff and his pupils exceptional high timekeeping standards. His reputation is valued that much by his peers that he is invited to give a key note address at a head teachers' conference. Unfortunately, he catches the wrong train and misses his connection. The rest of the film is taken up by a series of riotous events as Stimpson tries to make the conference on time. Does he do it? Watch the film to find out. It should be part of every time-obsessive manager's training programme.

Hot Tip: Time is your most precious commodity – use it properly.

The final word on managing time:

- Start by keeping a record of the interruption; who interrupted you, the degree of importance attached to the interruption and how long the whole interaction lasted.
- Analyse whether the interruption was valid. Ask whether it needed to be dealt with immediately or could have been delayed or avoided.

- Accept that some interruptions are necessary and require urgent action.
- Appreciate that although the interruption may be of low importance/urgency to you, it may not be this way for the person interrupting you.
- Learn to say 'No'. Doing this in a polite and courteous manner followed by a short explanation is the assertive way of dealing with an interruption.
- An important part of the leadership role is to be available to people, to deal with important issues and to make your staff as effective as possible.
- Giving unlimited access to your time will prevent you from dealing with important issues.
- Imposing barriers to accessibility that are too high, however, will also prevent you from dealing with important issues.
- Time is your most precious commodity – use it properly.

SUMMARY: A TRUE STORY

THE DECK OF CARDS (WITH APOLOGIES TO T. TEXAS TYLER)

Some time ago, during an important Ofsted inspection, a young head teacher, new to the role, was seen playing with a pack of playing cards when he should have been listening to the Ofsted Chief Inspector's briefing. When the Chief Inspector took him to one side and threatened to report him to the school governors, the young head teacher replied meekly that he knew of the importance of the inspection to the school and also that he was shortly to be interrogated by Ofsted.

Unfortunately, he had forgotten to bring his copies of the Ofsted guide to school inspection or Bush and Middlewood's *Leading and Managing People in Education* with him to the inspection. Lost without these books, he turned to his pack of cards for inspiration and told the Chief Inspector that:

- 'When I look at the **Ace** it reminds me of the singularity of the vision that drives the school. The Ace is also both the lowest and highest card in the pack, which reminds me that leadership may require either a top-down or bottom-up approach depending on the circumstances.'
- 'The **deuce** reminds me of the two attributes that underpin good leadership; flexibility and determination.'
- 'The **three** stands for the three components that make up the project triangle: quality, time and cost.'
- 'The **four** relates to Handy's four gods of culture: Apollo, Zeus, Athena and Dionysus.'
- 'The **five** reminds me of the five phases in Kübler-Ross's effects of change model: denial, anger, bargaining, depression and acceptance. The **five** also stands for the five phases in Tuckman's team development model: forming, norming, storming, performing and adjourning.'
- 'The **six** are Kipling's six honest serving-men who provide the questions we need to answer in any curriculum planning process: *What? Why? When? How? Where? Who?*'
- 'The **seven** stands for the *Seven Cs of Why* which make up the qualities needed to be a good leader (Creative, Courageous, Challenging, Communicative, Confident, Considerate and Calm).'

- 'The **eight** is the number of factors in the combined SWOT and PEST analyses that are important in establishing the feasibility of the school plan: SWOT (strengths, weaknesses, opportunities, threats) and PEST (political, economical, social, technical).'
- 'The **nine** reminds me of that there are nine roles that make up Belbin's effective team mix: coordinator, shaper, plant, monitor evaluator, implementer, resource investigator, team worker, completer finisher and specialist.'
- 'The **ten** reminds me of the ten psychopathic traits that I may find in my class and also reminds me that I could have any one or combination of these traits.'
- 'I'm stuck when I look at the **Jack**. This makes me realise that I don't have all the answers and will need to use the experience and knowledge of all members of the school. There are two one-eyed Jacks in the pack who make me think that some Ofsted inspectors take a blinkered approach when it comes to assessing school performance.'
- 'When I look at the **Queen** I'm reminded of the great Freddie Mercury and the lyrics to *Don't Stop Me Now*. These lyrics convince me that my school has unlimited potential and helping it to realise this can be a rewarding and pleasurable experience.'
- 'The **King** reminds me of Robert the Bruce, who reigned as the King of Scotland from 1306 to 1329, and the allegory that I learned at school about the spider attempting to spin its web. This allegory gives me the encouragement I need to persevere with the school, even if things aren't going to plan.'

'So you see sir, I wasn't gambling with my cards,' the young head teacher told the Chief Inspector, 'I was using them to inspire me to lead the school to the very best of my ability.' Unfortunately, the Chief Inspector was a country and western fan and remembered Wink Martindale's rendition of the song. The school was given a grade 4 for Leadership and Management for tarnishing Wink's name and failed its inspection. It went into special measures and the young head teacher went on to make a fortune on the poker circuit.

This may not exactly be the truth but why spoil a good story with the truth?

REFERENCES

Adair, J. (1983) *Effective Leadership: A modern guide to developing leadership skills*. London: Pan.

Adams, R. (2014) 'Findings of the Kershaw report into Birmingham's "Trojan horse" schools', *Guardian*, 18 July. Available at www.theguardian.com/uk-news/2014/jul/18/birmingham-trojan-horse-schools-report-findings (accessed 13/05/2107).

Adams, S. (1996) *The Dilbert Principle*. New York: HarperCollins.

Argyris, C. and Schön, D. (2002) *Theory in Practice*. San Francisco, CA: Jossey-Bass.

Ashby, W. R. (1956) *An Introduction to Cybernetics*. London: Chapman & Hall.

Bandler, R. and Grinder, J. (1979) *Frogs into Princes: Introduction to neurolinguistic programming*. Boulder, CO: Real People Press.

Barber, M., Moffit, A. and Kihn, P. (2010) *Deliverology 101*. London: Corwin.

Batchelor, M. (2010) *Project Management Secrets*. London: HarperCollins.

Bates, B. (2015) *The Little Book of Big Coaching Theories*. London: Pearsons.

Belbin, R. M. (1981) *Management Teams: Why they succeed or fail*. London: Heineman.

Bell, C. (2002) *Managers as Mentors*. San Francisco, CA: Berrett-Koehler.

Bentley, H., O'Hagan, O., Raff, A. and Bhatti, I. (2016) *How Safe Are Our Children?* London: NSPCC.

Berne, E. (2010 [1964]) *The Games People Play: The psychology of human relationships*. London: Penguin.

Bolman, L. G. and Deal, T. E. (2008) *Reframing Organizations: Artistry, choice, and leadership*. San Francisco, CA: Jossey-Bass.

Bryk, A. S. and Schneider, B.L. (2002) *Trust in Schools*. New York: Russell Sage Foundation.

Burns, J. M. (1978) *Leadership*. New York: Harper & Row.

Bush, T. and Middlewood, D. (2006) *Leading and Managing People in Education*. London: Sage.

Costa, A. and Kallick, B. (1983) 'Through the lens of a critical friend', *Educational Leadership*, 51 (2): 49–51.

Covey, S. (2004) *The 7 Habits of Highly Effective People*. London: Simon & Schuster.

Crosby, P. (1980) *Quality is Free*. London: Penguin.

De Bono, E. (2009) *Six Thinking Hats*. London: Penguin.

Deming, W. E. (2000) *Out of Crisis*. Cambridge, MA: MIT.

Department for Education (DfE) (2015a) *Protecting Children from Radicalisation: The prevent duty*. London: DfE.

Department for Education (DfE) (2015b) *National Standards of Excellence for Headteachers*. London: DfE.

Department for Education (DfE) (2015c) *The Prevent Duty: Departmental advice for schools and childcare providers*. London: DfE.

Department for Education (DfE) (2016) *Keeping Children Safe in Education*. London: DfE.

Egan, G. (1994) *Working the Shadow Side: A guide to positive behind-the-scenes management*. New York: Wiley.

Fiedler, F. E. (1967) *A Theory of Leadership Effectiveness*. New York: McGraw-Hill.

Fisher, J. (2012) 'Fisher transition curve'. Available at https://www.csu.edu.au/__data/assets/pdf_file/0006/949533/fisher-transition-curve-2012.pdf (accessed 13/07/2017).

French, J. R. P. and Raven, B. (1959) 'The bases of social power', in D. Cartwright (ed.), *Studies in Social Power*. Ann Arbor, MI: University of Michigan.

Gibb, C. A. (1958) 'An interactional view of the emergence of leadership', in C. A. Gibb (1969) (ed.), *Leadership*. Harmondsworth: Penguin.

Goleman, D. (1996) *Emotional Intelligence: Why it can matter more than IQ*. London: Bloomsbury.

Handy, C. (1993) *Understanding Organisations*. London: Penguin.

Handy, C. (2011) *The Gods of Management: The changing work of organisations*. London: Souvenir Press.

Hare, R. D. (2003) *The Psychopathic Checklist* (2nd edn). Toronto: Multi-Health Systems.

Henshaw, P. (2016) 'Heads Up campaign encourages the headteachers of the future', *SecEd*, 27 January. Available at www.sec-ed.co.uk/news/heads-up-campaign-encourages-the-head-teachers-of-the-future/ (accessed 13/05/2107).

Hersey, P. and Blanchard, K. H. (1969) *Management of Organizational Behavior: Utilizing human resources*. Englewood Cliffs, NJ: Prentice Hall.

Herzberg, F., Mausner, B. and Snyderman, B. B. (2011) *Organization and Business – Vol. 1: The Motivation to Work*. New York: Transaction.

Homans, G. C. (1958) 'Social behavior as exchange', *American Journal of Sociology*, 63 (6): 597–606.

Johnson, J. and Scholes, K. (2002) *Exploring Corporate Strategy* (7th edn). London: Financial Times/Prentice Hall.

Juran, J. (1967) *Management of Quality Control*. New York: McGraw-Hill.

Kabat-Zinn, J. (1994) *Wherever You Go, There You Are*. New York: Hyperion.

Kandola, R. and Fullerton, J. (2003) *Diversity in Action: Managing the mosaic*. Trowbridge: Cromwell Press.

Karpman, S. (1968) 'Fairy tales and script drama analysis', *Transactional Analysis Bulletin*, 26 (7): 39–43.

Kübler-Ross, E. (2005) *On Grief and Grieving: Finding the meaning of grief through the five stages of loss*. New York: Simon & Schuster.

Kumra, S. and Manfredi, S. (2012) *Managing Equality and Diversity: Theory and practice*. Oxford: Oxford University Press.

Lasswell, H. (1979) *Propaganda and Communication in World History*. Honolulu, HI: University of Hawaii Press.

Lewin, K. (1935) *A Dynamic Theory of Personality*. New York: McGraw-Hill.

MacGregor Burns, J. (1978) *Leadership*. New York: Harper & Row.

Machiavelli, N. (2004) *Penguin Great Ideas: The Prince*. London: Penguin.

Maslow, A. H. (1987) *Motivation and Personality* (3rd edn). New York: HarperCollins.

McGrath, J. and Bates, B. (2013) *The Little Book of Big Management Theories*. London: Pearsons.

McGrath, J. and Bates, B. (2017) *The Little Book of Big Management Theories* (2nd edn). London: Pearsons.

McGregor, D. (2006) *The Human Side of Enterprise*. New York: McGraw-Hill.

Moorhead, J. (2012) 'Who'd be a headteacher in 2012?', *Guardian*, 20 February. Available at www.theguardian.com/education/2012/feb/20/headteacher-recruitment-more-difficult (accessed 13/05/2017).

Morgan, G. (2006) *Images of Organisations*. London: Sage.

Neill, A. S. (1960) *Summerhill School: A radical approach to learning*. New York: St. Martin's Griffin.

Pedlar, M., Burgoyne, J. and Boydell, T. (1997) *The Learning Company* (2nd edn). Basingstoke: McGraw-Hill.

Peter, L. J. and Hull, R. (2009) *The Peter Principle*. New York: HarperCollins.

Press Association (2016) 'English schools "may face shortage of 19,000 heads by 2022', *Guardian*, 11 November. Available at www.theguardian.com/education/2016/nov/11/english-schools-shortage-of-19000-heads-by-2022-report (accessed 13/05/2017).

Ronson, J. (2011) *The Psychopath Test*. London: Picador.

Schein, E. (1985) *Organisational Culture and Leadership*. San Francisco, CA: Jossey-Bass.

Steinhoff, C. R. and Owens, R. G. (1989) 'The organizational culture assessment inventory: A metaphorical analysis in educational settings', *Journal of Educational Administration*, 27: 17–23.

Taylor, F. W. *(1911) The Principles of Scientific Management*. New York: Harper & Brothers.

Thomas, K. W. and Kilmann, R. H. (1974) *Thomas-Kilmann Conflict Model Instrument*. New York: Xicom.

Tuckman, B. W. (1965) 'Development sequences in small groups', *Psychology Bulletin*, 3 (6): 384–99.

West-Burnham, J. and Harris, D. (2015) *Leadership Dialogues*. Camarthen: Crown House.

Wheelan, S. A. (2013) *Creating Effective Teams*. London: Sage.

Whitmore, J. (1998) *Coaching for Performance*. London: Nicholas Brealey.

INDEX